From Cornish Roots

Marlene May

Edward Gaskell
DEVON

First published 2015
Edward Gaskell publishers
Park Cottage
East-the-Water
Bideford
Devon
EX39 4AS

ISBN 978-1-906769-57-4

From
Cornish
Roots

Marlene May

Typeset, printed and bound by
Lazarus Press
Caddsdown Business Park
Bideford
Devon
EX39 3DX
www.lazaruspress.com

Foreword

The purpose of this book is to enlighten my future generation a little about their roots. I never kept a diary, these are just some events I remember from my past. Love and dedication to my family: Donald my husband, Elysia and Tracey my daughters, and Jade, Chloe and Ben my grandchildren.

Lazarus Press
Bideford
DEVON
www.lazaruspress.com

Jade's 13th birthday party.

Edward Gaskell
publishers
DEVON

1

Let me begin my story by returning to my roots, going back through three generations. My name was Marlene Cann, and I was born on 6th April 1937 (my name change comes later in the book).

I was born in the little village of Fraddon in Cornwall. Although I was only 8 years old when my great grandparents died I still remember so much about them, however to go back further than my memory allows needed considerable research. My great grandfather Edward White, was the eldest of three boys, Richard and William being the others, who were born in County Wexford in Ireland. Times were hard in Ireland at this time so they decided to hopefully make a better life in England. Edward would have been about 20 years old. I haven't found much information on William other than that, with his brothers he decided to come to the West Country, specifically the St. Stephen/Meledor area.

Richard and Edward both found employment on the Great Western Railway line. Edward was an engine man while William was a packer for the line. Edward later left to take over a smallholding, farming on Meledor Moors. Meledor was just a little hamlet in the district of Stephens/ Trevisco. Clay working was the only means of work apart from agriculture and great grandfather's farm fell victim to the associated mining, field after field disappearing until the day the house fell also.

He was compensated by the china clay industry, but his home had gone. He moved into the community of Meledor, just a small hamlet of a few houses and a school. Meledor has been long gone, wiped off the map as the clay mining gradually tore away the landscape. The great white mountains of clay that could be seen for miles were all that were left behind. The pits filled with water and looked like blue lakes. The 'Eden Project' has now sprung up on that landscape. The mountains of clay now after many years have become green, overgrown with vegetation.

I believe Richard and William married two sisters from Trethosa. Richard and his wife went on to have a daughter, May, and with his family decided to venture further and emigrated to San Bernardino in California in 1879. He did very well and went on to own an orange plantation. It was all shortly after the gold rush days, and things were very rough. Shanty towns had sprung up along with gold mining fever.

I visited May, his daughter, in 1966 and she told me stories of their life out there. Their house in the early days was down a long lane which was pitted with cartwheel tracks from the wagons and horses. It was hoped the horses wouldn't tread on one of the rattlesnakes that crept into the grooves on the road for warmth from the sun, and get bitten on their legs. After many years, Richard came back with his daughter to England for a visit during which time they also visited his native Ireland. They did only visit once as travel was too expensive.

Prior to Richard emigrating to America my great grandfather Edward had met and married my great grandmother Ellen Allen who previously lived in the Nanpean/St Stephens area. They married in St Stephen's registry office in July 1874. She had been a clay worker, and was five years older than Edward. She could neither read nor write and had to put an 'x' on their marriage certificate.

They went on to have five children. William Thomas the eldest (my grandfather) born 1875, Amanda Clocena next, who died at the age of 26 years old, and next Agnes Jane, followed by Draxey Mabel, with Arthur the youngest. Arthur became a soldier in the first world war. He was so traumatised by what he saw and went through that when at last he

Above: My maternal great grandparents Edward and Ellen White at their home in Meledor.

Left: Mum and myself at greatgrandparents home in 1941 at Meledor. I'm about 4 years old.

Above: Grandpa, second from the left, and his work colleagues building our house at Fraddon

Right: Me with great-grandpa Edward White at Fraddon. Grandpa is at the back.

came home he was shell shocked and suffered what in those days was called 'a nervous breakdown' but what they might nowadays, in more enlightened times, refer to as 'post traumatic stress disorder'. He spent some time having treatment in the mental hospital in Bodmin before he returned to his family.

Edward worked until he was 70 years old, and was quoted as saying he wished he had never retired, because 'work keeps a man going and is good for one'. He was also quoted as saying he loved walking miles and miles, and thought people would be a lot healthier if they did the same. Edward and Ellen had 19 grandchildren and 18 great-grandchildren. Ellen had some kind of accident five years before she died, fracturing her leg. They both lived to a great age: Ellen 97 and Edward 92 years. Hard work and plain living paid off.

They died within a week of each other, everyone said it was through grief as they were so devoted to each other.

Now the next generation down, to my grandfather William Thomas White. He met my grandmother Ellen Bullock, they married, and went on to have three children. Ivy Clocena (my mother) Leda Amanda, and Edward (Eddie).

I was born in my maternal grandparents' house next door to the house where I would be spending a good deal of my younger days in a small village called Fraddon in Cornwall. My life consisted of my grandpa, grandma, Aunty Leda, mum and dad and two younger sisters, Gloria and Barbara. We lived next door to my grandparents in one of a pair of semi-detached houses both of which my grandpa had helped to build and he now owned. I remember cycling with my mum down dusty, clay lanes to Meledor about a three mile journey. The road ran between the pits, and I remember seeing the trollies running up and down the mountains of clay on tracks, taking the waste from the mines and tipping out at the top. It was a never-ending journey one trolly going up and one coming down. Mum had lived in that environment until leaving school with her siblings.

I remember visiting my great grandparents whose house was very stark and old fashioned with stone floors and no mats. In the kitchen there was a very high mantle piece, on which were several china dogs, over a black leaded stove. The stove used for heating and cooking, had to be stoked up with coal. Situated in front was a high backed settle as hard as the pews in church - a long way from the settees we have today. They had a beautiful little canary, which always sang so sweetly, such a joy.They also had a wind up gramophone with a big horn - it might have been called 'His Master's Voice - which they often used to play. The lavatory was at the top of the long garden; no modern contraption just a little wooden hut with a wooden bench and a hole with a bucket underneath. Squares of cut-up newspapers on a string served for toilet paper. It didn't seem primitive at the time.

My grandma and grandpa and family having moved to Fraddon many years on, were now living a more modern lifestyle. Mum and Aunty Leda after they left school went to work as machinists in a knitting factory in Newquay. Mum at this point bought herself a Royal Enfield motor bike which gave her and Aunty Leda much more freedom - there was very little traffic on the roads. Grandpa said he could hear her bike coming home about three miles away, as the roads were so quiet.

Uncle Eddie decided to join the Royal Navy as a young rating, serving on ships during the second world war: one ship I remember him being on was HMS *Rodney*. He served thirty years in all and worked his way up to sub-lieutenant. During this time he had met and married May Bettis from Lee Moore, Plymouth,and that is where they settled. Later their son - my cousin Graham - was born, and their lives would be part of my growing up. Probably Uncle Eddie had followed the tradition of his father (my grandpa) into the navy. Grandpa's young life was in the Royal Navy when he was first married. He was a stoker in the engine room on board ship. He spent some time in the far east, and brought home lots of oriental things. Some of those beautiful china tea-sets have been passes down to me. It was when he left the sea that he took up in the building trade.

Grandma on the other hand, before they were married used to work 'in service' as a housemaid - which a lot of other young women did in those days. She told me once about a young family she worked for in Falmouth, to whom strange things used to happen at night. She used to put the children to bed and when they woke in the morning their nightclothes were always back to front. Also about pictures that slipped off the wall, the string and nail still intact. She said there was something definitely spooky about that house.

Life must have been hard for grandma and grandpa but they were happy raising their family. They also had a built-in stove that had to be stoked with coal.The oven for baking and roasting, and the rings on top for heating water: it was kept burning twenty four hours a day, seven days a week. So it was always warm in the living room. The stove was kept smart by blackleading it. The heating in the sitting-room was from an open grate. The main bedroom also had an open grate which was rarely used as it used to smoke, probably because of birds' nests in the chimney. This was the very room years later that I was born in.

Ironing was done on the kitchen table. The iron was a flat iron which had to be heated on top of the stove. There wasn't a carpet in the house, apart from on the stairs. All the rooms were laid with lino. There were lots of rag mats which my grandma used to make. The stair-carpet had to be brushed by hand, and all the dust went up your nose - no such thing then as a vacuum cleaner. They had lots of stuffed birds in glass cases on the wall in the living room and the three piece suite in the front room, which was very hard and uncomfortable, was there from as far back as I can remember: when I was about three years old. It was still there when we had to clear the house after Aunty Leda died. I was then in my forties. I adored my grandpa and remember following him around, and him taking me for walks to the village shop for sweets. He was a very quiet and patient man and spent ages allowing me to brush and combe his hair. He had a beautiful African green parrot that used to talk a lot and say such things as 'Pretty Polly', 'Polly want Potato' and 'Come on Leda' when he knew it was time for Aunt Leda to arrive home from work. Grandpa used to let him out of the cage at times and perch on his shoulders, but I used to disappear at that point, as I didn't fancy testing out his pecking skills.

When I was a child one of the two little shops in the village was actually the front room of a house. This was a time when most things had to be purchased with ration coupons. A lot of the time people felt lucky to obtain a fresh egg, mostly having to put up with dried powder eggs. Still the little shop in the front room was always stocked with most things needed. The other regular shop further up the village was owned and run by an eccentric man and his even stranger son. Once, when grandpa took me in to the shop, I was greeted with, 'Hello, little boy!'. To which I indignantly replied, 'I am *not* a little boy.' Sometimes he would say, 'Sing me a song and I'll give you sixpence'. I flatly refused. Things like this happened every time I was taken into the shop. Years later - thirty years or more, and after the father had passed on - the son was found dead in suspicious circumstances inside the house. The police never solved the case.

Most everything was rationed, and everyone had ration books and clothing coupons. Many clothes were made out of blankets: coats mostly. Dresses and underwear made from parachute silk. Aunt Leda at this time was a dressmaker, a very good one, and it was nice having one in the family as she made a lot of our clothes. Times were hard. A lot of people in our village used to come to her and she built up quite a good business, eventually making a good living from it. She prefered working at home rather than going out, as unfortunately she didn't enjoy good health. She was born without a cup bone in her hip, making her lame. Needless to say she spent all her life in and out of hospital, having numerous operations, and in constant pain. It would have been a different thing in this day and age. Through therapy at Truro hospital she learnt to make soft toys - every animal under the sun - and very professionally done. She never married, but chose to stay and look after her parents, although she had the chance to marry and go to Canada.

Grandma used to wear long dresses that swept the ground and always an apron to cover. She was a very stout woman and very hard working. Wash days were always on a Monday and was hard work taking all day to do the family wash by hand: no washing machines in those days. It was all done in a tin bath in the out-house, two washes and a Reckits blue rinse. Eventually using a wringer and a mangle when the sheets were dry for pressing. Grandpa made me my own little washing line so I could hang out the hankies and dolls clothes.

Our house had three bedrooms, bathroom and three rooms downstairs,it was a fairly spacious house. We had no mains water connected (that came much later) but we used the water from our well in our back garden, pumped in with a little hand pump connected over the kitchen sink. When we wanted a bath mum had to heat the water in an electric burco boiler, in the back kitchen and carry it upstairs in buckets. Sometimes when we were small mum bathed us in front of the fire in the kitchen in a tin bath - yes, the same tin bath from the outhouse. When I was old enough I had to help mum with washdays. It was hard on the hands. I think all the lifting of the full baths of water in order to empty them over the years resulted in mum having to go into hospital with a badly twisted womb. We didn't have central heating we had open grate fires in both rooms, so you can imagine the bedrooms were very cold in winter. Still we cuddled up in a feather mattress and hot water bottles at night, and a potty under the bed. Our 'fridge' was situated outside, consisting of a wooden cabinet, the front covered with mesh, which kept our food reasonably cold, and this we called 'our safe'. We had large gardens in the back to both houses, and a well. The water from the well, which served both houses, was always so cool and sweet. It wasn't until many years later we had the mains supplied. The seasons of the year seemed so very different then: the winters so cold and the summers so hot. Mum never let us out of our winter clothes until the end of May. She used to say, 'Never cast a clout till May is out'm, irespective of what the temperature was. Winters were not only bitterly cold and wet, but many times we were snowed in for what seemed weeks. I used to suffer with chilblains,my fingers and toes swollen.

Summers seemed always long and hot, and as children we loved joining in the haymaking in the field behind our house. Best part was getting to ride on the tractor and trailer. Summer-time I loved, we had so much to do, picking blackberries and mum preserving fruits and making jams and tarts. She used to take us up on the downs, just up the road from our house, to pick what we called erts (a kind of blueberry) from bushes that covered the ground. We had to be careful to look out for snakes. Mum was such a good cook, baking all her own bread and cakes. The smell of fresh bread was delicious and mouth watering and we couldn't wait to cut and butter it. Saffron and caraway seed cakes were good.

On the savoury side her potato cakes and fish cakes were scrumptious: good wholesome food, it makes me hungry just to think back.

I used to love to help mum in the kitchen. Besides the cooking of cakes and pastries, she taught me how to gut fish. Not something I liked doing very much, but if it's done quickly it's not too bad. Also how to skin and prepare a rabbit for the dinner table. Rabbit was very often on the menu, and very tasty.

There was a door to door delivery of fresh milk every day, from a farmer who used to carry churns of milk in his van. He would measure it out and bring it into the house loose and tip it into mum's jugs. The co-op would deliver all our groceries once a week. A butcher would arrive also once a week and mum could choose whatever cut of meat she wanted, as it was a walk-in butcher's van.

A fish man would arrive on Fridays again with a variety of fish. Also the 'Corona' lorry came once a week, with all the bottles of pop. American cream soda, dandelion and burdock, ginger beer and all the usual favourites.The bottles had ball top clip-on, and were returnable at tuppence a bottle.

We had a happy childhood especially with our grandparents living next door. We spent as much time with them as we did in our own house.

Grandma was quite religious, on Sundays we weren't allowed to knit or sew or play cards as she said it was sinful.

Seeing as my dad was away so much in the Fleet Air Arm, grandpa used to till both gardens which he seemed to enjoy. We grew all kinds of vegetables, fruit trees and fruit bushes - we didn't have to buy any. When I think back it was so good, and I was happy that as a child I could escape into play, while the grown-ups were hard at work. Grandpa kept about a dozen chickens, so we also had fresh eggs, plus the occasional chicken dinner.

Mum and dad had met while she and Aunt Leda were staying with friends in Margate in Kent. Dad was stationed there at RAF Manson.They stayed there a month or so,then mum found she was pregnant with me. So they hurriedly got married. My grandparents took an instant dislike to him and they couldn't get on. So my parents' marriage had gotten off on the wrong footing. They never forgave him for getting their daughter pregnant. My mum came back home to live while dad continued to serve in the RAF away from home. He was still in the RAF when I was born before he made the change to the Fleet Air Arm. His job was A/E (air engineer) and he was away nearly all the time, serving 22 years stationed in various camps, mostly home bases apart from on board ships to Malta and Long Beach, California, and one posting to Northern Ireland.

I used to enjoy air days on his bases at Culdrose, St Merryn, or navy days at Plymouth. One trip he took us on while in uniform, was to Plymouth Navy Days, and I was taken ill with terrible tummy pains on HMS *Ocean* (his serving ship).

He took me down into the sick bay where the navy doctor diagnosed me with food poisoning and treated me.

Something very frightening happened to me at the age of eight. We were having our evening meal (I remember it was pasties) when I started coughing up blood,and couldn't stop. The doctor was called out, who then immediately called an ambulance and I was rushed into the isolation hospital in Truro, as they thought I must have something contagious. Days later they transfered me to the city hospital for treatment. I was diagnosed with an abscess on one of my lungs. It turned out to be a four month stay in hospital, including Christmas. Not being sure how to treat me, the doctors decided to try penicillin. The drug not widely used then.The doctors told mum they weren't sure it would work on me, but would give it a try. I was treated with injections every four hours, day and night in my arms and in my legs - anywhere they could find a piece of flesh not already punctured, until I looked and felt like a pincushion. I remember one nurse giving me an injection above the knee, and it felt like my leg was burning and I was crying because it hurt so much. At one point I was taken down to operating theatre, where I had four injections in my throat before having a chest X-ray. I wasn't aware until years later how really ill I had been - I was told it was touch and go, but thank goodness for penicillin which saved my life. How research and medicine has improved since those days. During my stay in hospital I was allowed to paint in bed and make any amount of mess, and the nurses didn't appear to mind - I quite enjoyed it, not knowing there was a possibility I could have died.

That Christmas in hospital was made wonderful for everyone in the ward. I remember a big tree in the ward and life-size figures of snow white and the seven dwarfs around the tree. Father Christmas came to visit us all, but really I knew it was Dr Andrews as I recognised his brown shoes. One evening there was a staff party and the nurses all came around the ward one by one, showing off their lovely evening dresses. Then they turned their capes inside out with the red lining showing and, each having lanterns, went around the hospital singing carols. Visitors were allowed to come in and see me anytime, and there were no restrictions. Mum came every morning and caught the last bus home at night, believing as everyone knew except me that I wasn't expected to live. Anyway I proved to be a hardy, tough little girl and after four months was allowed to go home.

I wasn't though, able to return to school for months as I had to recuperate and this, in turn, put me behind in all my lessons at school.

When I came home from hospital all the curtains were drawn. No-one told me but I knew right away what had happened and whispered, 'Great grandparents have died haven't they?'

Pre-school years I had been a lonely child, only having grown-ups for company, so I had to look to my own devices to amuse myself. Outside grandma's back door hung on the wall was a horseshoe for luck (very rusty) and I kept poking it with a stick, though I was repeatedly told to stop. It came off and landed on my forehead cutting it badly. I had to have medical treatment as it was so rusty and I still bear the scar as a tribute . Going to school at five years old was the first time I had really associated with other children and I was quite shy. Our village school was a two mile walk every day to and from. It was just one school and we attended it from ages 5-15 years unless you passed the 11 plus exam and qualified to attend the Grammar School at Newquay. Needless to say after having had about a year off school between the ages 8 and 9, I had fallen behind with my lessons, didn't catch up, and never did pass my 11 plus. However I worked hard and enjoyed my later school years.

Gloria my younger sister did pass her 11 plus when it came to her turn, so she enjoyed a different environment. On the whole I didn't like school very much early on, and made excuses to stay at home whenever I could, only to have the school attendance officer once call on mum. Mum used to keep a little 'withy stick' tucked behind a picture and if we were naughty 'look out!', we'd feel the stick against our legs. We'd see it coming and take flight, and mum would chase me down the road with it mostly because I didn't want to go to school.

I remember snippets of the second world war years, mum waking me some nights when there were air raids often overshooting their target at Plymouth Dockyards, and enemy aircraft were around. We would go downstairs to the kitchen and sit under the big table in case of flying glass should a window be blown out. Luckily no bombs were dropped near us and the nearest airfields were St Mawgan, St Merryn, and St Eval about 12 miles away, although there was an electricity sub station near our village. At the air bases were housed four-engine lancasters, and they were often flying over our house. Our area was the turn-about point for them, as they circled back to base. There was always the slow heavy drawl of the engines, during and just after the war.

Once while we were staying with friends of my parents in Cannock, Staffs there was an air raid. Only being about 4 years old I thought it was great fun to rush down to the cellar until it was all over, taking torches and flasks. My sister Gloria was born on 4th Oct 1942 when I was 5 years old. She was born at home. I remember she had quite a head of dark hair. When there were air raids, and the risk of chemical gas poisoning, she would have to be put in an incubator type contraption to isolate her from any gas fumes. Lucky enough it never had to be used. Everyone had to carry a gas mask around with them in a little box carried like a shoulder bag.

The gas masks looked quite horrible, like something out of star wars, again luckily enough we never had to wear them, but there was always that risk.

There was a large tented camp at lower Fraddon where American soldiers were billeted. The village was all hustle and bustle with their tanks and jeeps driving around. A lot of local people did the laundry of their shirts. A few of them came to Aunt Leda for their sewing. The Village Hall was used to welcome them with social events, dances and whist drives. Mum used to take us by train to Plymouth sometimes where we would meet up with Aunty May and Graham to go shopping. We met up at Christmas-times for the pantomime in the Theatre Royal and these events were always looked forward to. A large part of Plymouth had been bombed badly and there were quite a lot of ruins. Plymouth was a prime target as the Germans were after bombing the naval dockyard.

We had to travel everywhere by public transport as we didn't have a car. Only the well-off had cars and in Cornwall that wasn't many. Needless to say the trains and buses were always full. When we were taken to the beach in Newquay it was quite a day out. Firstly we had to walk about a mile to catch the train to Newquay with all our buckets and spades and food for the day.

At one point Gloria and myself had to go into hospital at St Austell to each have a tooth taken out. Mine had an abscess on the gum. Gloria went first and was so quick, a whiff of ether and out - she was sitting up in the nurse's arms when she came out of the theatre. Mine took longer, and I took fright when I saw the ether mask coming towards me to cover my face, and... boy I fought! I was terrified, and fought until I lost consciousness. The doctor remarked to mum afterwards, 'You've got a real soldier there - she fought to the last.'

Grandpa used to go down to the moors for hours on end to pick hazel nuts, so we always had a nice stock in for Christmas. Just before Christmas Eve he would again go down to the moors, and cut us a Christmas Tree. It was always holly, we never had fir, you can imagine it was quite prickly to decorate. Our christmases were always quite wonderful. We were never allowed to open our presents until after dinner, when grandpa and grandma would join us in our front room.

No-one had a TV, we used to listen to the radio a lot, especially kid's programmes like Dick Barton Special Agent and Dan Dare Pilot of the Future. Mum's knitting needles never stopped in the evenings, as we all listened to the radio.

We always seemed to have one cat after another. I remember one cat having fleas, and dad rubbing her coat in paraffin unfortunately this killed both the fleas and the cat. One cat had kittens and one of the family drowned them all - I was only young and was quite upset when I found out. Our dear cat Blackie we had for about 10 years or more. At one time he went missing for days, eventually coming home with an injured paw. It looked as though he had caught it in a gin trap. The farmers used to put these traps in the fields to catch rabbits. After that time Blackie was lame and walked with a limp.

My father (Edmund known as Eddie) had two brothers and a half-brother, Dad's surname being Cann. Grandma Garlick, as we called her, had married twice, her first husband (my paternal grandfather) having died. Dad's brothers were Herbert and Clary Cann; and Laurie Garlick. Home for them in their early years was Darlington, in County Durham - Andy Capp country. Grandma's second husband also died so we never knew him. We didn't see grandma Garlick very often which was just as well because mum didn't like her. She wore a ginger wig, as for some reason she had lost all her hair, and she smelled of cigarettes.

Her terraced house in the town was a two up two down, and lit by gas lamps on the wall so there was a permanent smell of gas mingled with cigarettes at all times. Mum hated visiting, she said there were dog hairs everywhere and grandma told smutty jokes. The terrier she had was called Mickey Dripping. When I was about 3 years old I wanted to get the attention of one of my uncle's while he was shaving in the kitchen sink. He was irritated and threw the whole pan of water over me, which angered mum. We didn't keep in touch with dad's side of the family later on after mum died.

My second sister Barbara was born on 19th Dec 1947, surprisingly, in a nursing home in Plymouth. I wonder now if it was because of an incident when mum was pregnant

She must have been about six months' pregnant, when mum and dad started arguing. They were always arguing, only this time it went a step too far and he hit her. She lost her balance and fell to the floor. I was about 10 years old at the time and was terrified of what he had done to mum. I rushed next door to get my grandparents.

They took over the situation and called the doctor, but luckily mum was OK. We didn't have a telephone so we always had to go down the village to use the public box.Very few people had their own telephone. Dad used to like a drink sometimes when he came home on leave and would go down to the local pub in the village.

Mum never went with him. She thought it was common for a woman to go in a pub. Grandma and Grandpa didn't approve of alcohol, so when dad came back that's when the arguments started. I do believe they were more involved than they should have been, looking out for their daughter. Maybe it's what becomes of living next door to your in-laws.

Dad being in the forces was away a lot - a foreign posting could be up to 2 years, not like the short stints they have today. Maybe it was just as well sometimes, as when he came home there always seemed to be a lot of arguments. He would finish up by packing his suitcase and leaving - walking down the road.

Mum always sent either me or Gloria after him begging him to come home, which invariably he did. This was always his solution to end the arguments.

During one row on a Sunday he got so mad he grabbed all the Sunday lunch that was cooking, all the saucepans of veg, and threw it all out into the garden. We didn't get any dinner that day. He always tried to make fun of me, right until I left home at 19 years old, saying personal things about me in front of people that embarrassed me. He took great delight in seeing me blush as at that age I was still very shy and quiet, so it made me feel very uncomfortable. One time when I was 10 or 11 years old I had been disobedient about something and he marched me up to my bedroom saying, 'I'm going to give you a good hiding!' I struggled but he put me across his knee and smacked my bare bum. By God, he was strong and he hit me hard: I couldn't sit down for a week. Another time he hit me across my head, slapping my ear so hard that I lost my hearing for several hours.

He used to say, 'You've got no brains, but you've got common sense.' To Gloria he used to say, 'You've got brains but *no* common sense.' Mum never stepped in - or that's how I remember it. Mum was a lovely lady, very gentle, and everyone liked her - she was very sociable. She liked whist drives and used to go regularly, especially the Christmas ones, and very often she was lucky, winning a goose or a turkey. I very often used to go with her, and I loved shopping in town with her. But I can't remember having any cuddles, though I suppose I must have had at times, and I have to remember her dedication and love when I was in Hospital and she came to see me every day. As children we all had to go to Sunday school and chapel every week at Indian Queens. I used to enjoy when the time came for what we called 'Chapel Summer Anniversary'. We had new outfits especially for the occasion, dress shoes and always new hat and gloves. The chapel was decorated with flowers. Us children were all in the choir seats and had a part to play singing and reciting. The following day, Monday, we had our anniversary tea which consisted of a mug of tea and a big saffron bun as big as a dinner plate. The tea was celebrated in a place called Queens Pit. It was a field circular in shape, cut grass tiers down on different levels like a amphitheatre. We used to sit on the bottom level for our tea, then afterwards we had great fun running around playing, while the brass band played, and the grown ups had their tea, more sedately on wooden trestle tables. The event was always crowed with parents and children.

Some summers when the weather was good the chapel services were held there on a Sunday evening. Mum used to push us into various things like the pantomimes in the village hall. Both Gloria and myself, had to reluctantly take

'Above: What we used to call 'Chapel Summer Anniversary'. The tea was celebrated in a place called Queens Pit at Indian Queens.

Left: Grandpa, Aunty Leda and me in their back garden - our garden was adjacent to the right.

Left: Hanging out my dollies and hankie washing. c1942

Right: Grandpa and Grandma, William and Ellen White.

Above: On the beach at Newquay myself, and sisters Barbara and Gloria, in the 1950s

Below: Mum and Dad on the beach at the same time.

Above: Mother Goose panto at Fraddon Village Hall

Left: My sister Gloria, Mum, and my sister Barbara.

part. I was also entered into music festivals in the village hall, when I had to play the piano and poetry recitations. Those days all the entertainment was home grown.

Gloria and myself had piano lessons which I quite enjoyed but she didn't. Gloria hated it and refused to practice. All Gloria wanted to do was to be allowed to have ballet lessons, but she wasn't allowed. We had to cycle about two miles to our tutor's house, for lessons, along a lonely desolate area of moorland, but I never felt scared in the dark. We went after school, so during the winter months it came in dark early. I should have mentioned earlier that Fraddon and Indian Queens are adjoining villages. I believe the latter received its name many years ago when Buffalo Bill was travelling around the country with his wild-west show - by all accounts they were in the area - and it was rumoured an Indian Queen stayed locally, so hence the name. Buffalo Bill employed a lot of native Americans in his shows.

My grandma (mum's mum) died, when I was about 13 years old, of stomach cancer. She endured quite a long and painful illness. As a younger woman she was a big, stout lady but her illness had torn away at her, and she was painfully thin when she passed away. Before the funeral was arranged she was laid to rest in the front room in an open coffin. Everyone paid their last respects to her. I was asked if I'd like to see her for the last time. It was the first time I'd seen a dead body and it put the fear of God into me, and upset me no end. There were no Chapel of Rests in those days, and the coffins had to be in the house before being buried. I refused to go into that room for ages afterwards as it gave me the creeps.

While dad was away in the navy mum decided to do a bit of bed/breakfast. The Newquay hotels used to get very full up in summer and visitors had begun to look outside the town, and even come out as far as Fraddon which was about 8 miles. Dad was not very keen on her doing it and used to say, 'You never know who you are taking into your home.' But mum enjoyed it and it was a bit of extra money. Everyone that stopped with us turned out to be really nice people and

Family day out to St Merryn Air display in the early 1950s. I am on the plane's wing, while standing is Gloria, Mum, and Barbara just in front of Dad.

asked to come back the following years. Indeed they became very good friends. Mum paid rent to grandpa of 7 shillings and sixpence per week (about 35 pence in today's money). Her weekly income was £7 per week paid to her from dad's naval money.

At 15 years of age it was time for me to leave school, and it felt, as it was, like a big step. Jobs were plentiful, I had many to choose from - and I had a number. I had no training of any kind and my first job was an ice cream packer which was good pay at £2-10/- per week (£2-50 in today's money) rising to £3. YIPPEE! At mum's suggestion I took a typing and shorthand course with a schoolteacher in the village who did evening classes in his house. I went on to get a job as an office junior in the factory at Newquay where mum had onced worked on the shop floor. But it wasn't my cup of tea, so I looked for something else. Next I worked in a garage as a forecourt attendant serving petrol. Still restless I yearned to move to something else and when I reached 16 years I

Myself and mum in the 1950s at Newquay.

wanted to leave home and be independent. I sent off for forms to join the navy - reasoning that I came from a line of naval personnel. I made the application and had an interview as well as a medical in Plymouth. I was accepted in my chosen category of cinema operator, and was given a date to join up. Unfortunately I chickened out and rejected the opportunity. I wasn't brave enough at that stage, unready to take the plunge. So it was back to the drawing board. I then got employment with the local co-op delivery service, which was when I learned to drive. I passed my test at 17 years.

With my first pay packet after leaving school, I was delighted that I could now buy my own clothes. It sticks in my mind that the very first item was a pair of red high heel shoes - the beginning of growing up and it felt good. I was now getting interested in speedway and used to go to the track at St Austell with friends. I loved the smell of the burnt cinder track, and the excitement of the race. I had one favourite St Austell (GULL) rider: a New Zealander called Allan Quinn. I used to hang around the pits to get autographs, especially the visitor riders. At one meeting a rider had a very bad accident and was taken into St Austell hospital. I really was so besotted with speedway and the riders that I made a point of visiting him in the hospital. God knows now when I look back on it, I must have been quite mad visiting a complete stranger. Young and foolish, I used to buy a speedway magazine on a regular basis and found inside people who wanted pen friends. I wrote to seven people one being in Australia, but it got too much,and I gradually let it peter out, apart from one boy called John. We met up when he came down from Little Lever in Manchester on his motor bike and stayed with us for a few days. I was invited back up to his house, it was the start of a friendship. While staying with John, he took me to Morecombe to see the sights, another evening to Blackpool to see the illuminations: it was fantastic. He would do anything for me, but he was more keen on me than I was on him; still, he was my first boyfriend. While staying with his family he took me to Southport. The beach there having a very long stretch of hard sand. A four seater aircraft was taking people on pleasure flights, I begged John to take me on a flight and although he was terrified, agreed. I enjoyed the flight so much, over the bay area. That was my first taste of flying, yet to me it wasn't adventurous *enough* - I wanted more. After the holiday and I went home, we wrote to each other for a while but in the end finished the friendship. My parents said I was a fool because he was such a nice lad. Quite coincidentally years later, I was living in Stafford and down on holiday in St Ives when who should I bump into but John who had a young lady with him: he introduced her to me as his wife. My past was catching up with me.

Dad was now stationed at RNAS Yeovilton, and phoned home to say someone on the camp was selling a car and he wanted to buy it. To get it home he needed a qualified driver with him as he was a learner - I was still a learner at that point myself. He asked mum to come up and bring it home with him, as she had a full licence, but she was ill in bed with a chill. Nevertheless she got up out of her sick bed and went to Yeovilton. While they were staying at a bed and breakfast he took her for an evening out and she foolishly left her cardigan behind. He wouldn't let her go back for it, and it was a chilly evening. Anyway we then were the proud owners of a car even if it was an old one and had seen better days. At that time there was no MOT nor checking on cars -I know the tyres on this one were rather smooth and the lights weren't very good. Still it got us around, and it made a change from riding on dad's motorbike and sidecar.

Mum got ill again with a chill virus which gradually got worse and she was taken into Truro hospital with double pneumonia. She had young student doctors drawing the fluid off her lungs by syringe which was very painful. While she was in hospital she said, 'I've got a feeling I'm never going home,' and told us what she wanted us to do with her things. We told her not to be so silly, talking like that. A week after she had been in, we got a phone call relayed by the post office in the village that mum had passed away. A post mortem showed a blood clot on her lungs. She had also shown the early signs of TB. Gloria, Barbara, and myself had to go to hospital to be tested, but we were all OK. Mum was brought home in a sealed coffin and had to rest in the front room before the funeral. I was devastated at losing mum, it hit me terribly hard as we had a very close relationship. Dad was due to retire shortly from the navy after 22 years and spend a bit of time at home, after all the years apart.

Mum was 47 years old and dad 42. Grandma Garlick came down to stay with us for a while, but she was of no earthly good to us. We girls wanted comfort, but we got none from her and were told instead to buck up and stop feeling sorry for ourselves. It's a good job we had grandpa and aunty Leda next door. Dad was granted a compassionate posting to RNAS Culdrose and used to come home most weekends. I kept my full time job with the Co-op and also kept house for myself and my two younger sisters, who were still at school, I was 18 and my sisters were 13 and 8. It was only a couple of months after mum died that dad picked up a girl at a dance on the camp. He brought her home to visit us and asked if I approved and asked did I like her. I told him I didn't like her and that anyway it was too soon. She took him to her home in St Ives to meet her parents, where he met her older sister Olive, who was more his age, and they started going out together. We kids were invited down to St Ives to spend Christmas with them all: a little bizarre to say the least. He followed through by marrying her the following year. So hence a new step-mum in a rather short space of time.

I never took to Olive. Before the marriage and when dad came home weekends, I used to go into Newquay, Saturday Night dancing in the Blue Lagoon with my friend Pat. One weekend dad took Pat and myself to a dance in the CPO's mess at Culdrose. During the evening he asked a Wren friend if she would take Pat and myself for a tour of the Wrens' quarters to give us an insight of naval life, as both Pat and myself were interested on possibly joining. I did enjoy the look around very much.

In the meantime while all of this was happening through the *Daily Mirror* newspaper I was writing to a guy at RAF Wildenrath in Germany. Another John, he was coming home to celebrate his 21st birthday and invited me up to his parents' home to stay for a party. This being in Rugeley near Stafford. Afterwards he came back home with me to Cornwall before going back to Germany, and so our friendship grew.

So now Dad married and went to live with his new wife in St Ives, and it was decided that Gloria and Barbara, being minors, would go with him. They were going to live with her parents as it was a big house and had plenty of room. Dad put all the household belongings into an auction and sold everything. I managed to salvage some photographs and some china. Of course Dad was glad to move away from Grandpa and Aunt Leda next door, as there was no love lost there and he did give me the option to move with them to St Ives, but I'd already decided on my future, and at 19 years of age decided to make the break. I couldn't accept Olive. Dad gave me the train fare for a one way ticket to Stafford: he'd got rid of me. So I moved to John's home territory: although he was still stationed in Germany, his parents welcomed me. I stayed with them for a couple of weeks until I got a job and a bed-sit in Stafford. I used to go over at weekends to see them, having bought a bicycle with which I'd cycle to and fro. The distance from Stafford to Rugeley was about nine miles. As I didn't know anyone, a couple of male friends of John's who did a lot of cycling asked me if I'd like to join them on various trips. They were nice lads and I enjoyed their company, cycling for miles. One weekend we went over to Alton Towers - it wasn't a theme park then - just a very big house with lovely gardens to wander around in. Anyway unknown to me at the time John's mother was writing to tell him I was gallivanting about the country with these lads and made it look bad for me. It all came out later when John came home from Germany on leave and was convinced one of them (Bill) was besotted with me which wasn't on my part. This relationship again wasn't meant to be so we called it a day.

At this stage, finishing with John and being so far away from home and no friends, I was terribly homesick. I asked dad if I could come home, but he refused. Never mind I'm now glad he did, although I didn't think so at the time. I've since never looked back and it was the making of me. I had to grow up and start fending for myself.

Meanwhile Gloria was having a hard time adjusting to her new life in St Ives. She wasn't happy and started to rebel. She went to Penzance Grammar School and by all accounts was doing very well. She wanted to carry on with her education but dad wouldn't listen to her. He took her out of school at 15 and told her to find a job. There was a point where she asked if she could come and live with me in Stafford, but I had to say no as I only had a bed sit and wasn't very happy myself at that moment in time. I moved to a number of bedsits in Stafford before I found the ideal one, having lot of ups and downs along the way, before I found the perfect one.

I began to feel happy again working as I'd done before on co-op on delivery vans, and stayed in that job for 4 years which was how long I stayed in Stafford. While I was in this job a lad, Fred, a work colleague , and I started dating. We dated for quite some time and talked of getting engaged, went dancing, visited cinemas: in all a very romantic time. Another of our leisure activities was cycling, which we did for miles each weekend. One time we cycled as far as Stratford-upon-Avon.

Soon, again, however the passion cooled and we decided to go our separate ways. I don't recall why, because it was quite a magical affair. I remember some lyrics from a song while we were going out, but can't remember the title or the singer, yet it still haunts me after all this time.

. . .Lanterns of gold
Lanterns of blue
Twinkle in the shadows
While I dance with you

An echo in the wind
Across the summer lane
Is sayin' you should know
That lanterns lose their glow
And hearts can break

So hold me close my darling
Then kiss me tenderly
And give your precious love
Your very precious love to me*

I think half the time I was attracted to good looking guys and in love with love. But I can look back with affection.

My 21st birthday was spent doing nothing special. Dad had sent me a cheque for £5 and Aunt Leda had sent me a lovely, big home-made iced birthday cake. She always looked out for me, and I always knew whatever happened her door would always be open; she helped me in every way possible.

It was while I was living at my last bed-sit with the 'Lunns' that I met and became great friends with a girl who like me, was on her own. Jean and I started a friendship that was to last more than 30 years. One particular Saturday night when we went to a dance - and at the time I wasn't dating anyone - a lad walked me home. We noticed someone walking a distance behind us: if we paused, this person paused and would drop back when we turned around. We came to the cul-de-sac where I lived and said bye, and went our separate ways. When out of the shadows came this figure towards me, he'd been following us all the way and now I was on my own he came after me. I ran for my life and too frightened to look for my keys I went straight to the front door and banged on it. The lights were still on and the people were up. As I made a lot of noise the man turned and ran off. My people had heard by then and opened the door and came out, but he had vanished. I was shaking like a leaf.

One Saturday night Jean and I met up with two lads who were friends, at a dance at Trentham Gardens,we were all

**A Very Precious Love* (1958) The Ames Brothers

there for the evening. The band was Joe Loss. Jean palled up with Bill and me with Ron (Ron being the one with the car). After that meeting we went out on foursomes every Saturday night, usually for a drink as most pubs had live music laid on. This went on for quite a long time, more than a year and always on foursomes, enjoying each others' company.

Summer came and our thoughts turned to holidays. I wanted to go abroad but Jean wasn't so keen, so I set off on my own. I'd booked with a coach company and had to travel via Dover for the ferry to Ostend. I hated that sea trip being sick as a dog all the way over. Our hotel destination was Ostend. The coach party were a very friendly crowd and I teamed up with a Chinese girl who was also on her own. We had quite a number of trips: Brussels was interesting and a beautiful city square with gold type buildings, and the famous *Manneken Pis* - a bronze sculpture depicting a naked little boy urinating into a fountain's basin. It was also the time of the world trade fare, and when the Atonium building was opened, a creation of metal balls rising to a 400 feet which housed restaurants, escalators, conference rooms and other public spaces.

We visited many places in both Holland and Belgium, including Bruges a small town, a little like Venice with all its canals and bridges where they make and sell beautiful lace. The highlight for me, though, was visiting Paris, and seeing the famous landmarks such as the Eiffel Tower, Arch De Triump and the beautiful Notre Dame Cathedral. There were so many lovely places to see, and we were able to watch the street artists painting. I only had a week there but such a lot crammed in. I enjoyed it immensely. When I came home Jean wanted to go to Butlins so I went along with it - not wholly enthusiastic. We went to Clacton-on-sea. It was different I suppose. We were still going out with Bill and Ron but these were girl holidays.

While I was still living in Stafford, my dear grandpa became very ill with bronchitis, and had to go into hospital. I got time off work and travelled down to Truro hospital to

My friend Jean and myself at Butlins in 1958.

Paris 1958 with a friend.

Right: The Eiffel Tower.

Left: At the Brussels trade exhibition and the Atomium.

visit him. I stayed for a few days but had to go back. It was after I got back days later, I received a telegram from Aunt Leda to say he was getting worse, but I couldn't get any more time off. One evening in my bedroom I had a premonition he had just died, I felt the relief of his suffering and stopped crying, because I knew it was all over. Next day I received a telegrammed to say he had passed away and about the time I had sensed it. I went home for the funeral and stayed at Aunt Leda's. When the reading of the will took place, Uncle Eddie was evil with the contents. Grandpa had left his house to Aunt Leda and the house next door in trust to us four grandchildren. Grandpa wanted Aunt Leda to keep her home. Uncle Eddie had enjoyed a good career and was well off financially whereas Aunt Leda on the other hand had nothing. Uncle Eddie was so furious that out of our sight he had hit Aunt Leda and knocked her down giving her a black eye.

He never did have any time for her, in my opinion all he was interested in was money.

Still on thoughts of premonitions, one night I had a dream I was being carried on a stretcher. I didn't think anymore about it until the following day when I was cycling down town for an appointment and was late, and was rushing. Out of the blue I turned for a split second and realised too late I was about to collide into a stationary vehicle. I was knocked unconscious. The next thing I remember was being carried into hospital on a stretcher, and everything I was seeing was exactly reliving my dream of the previous night.

Anyway Jean and Bill had got engaged and were preparing for their marriage.They had bought a house over in the Wednesbury/Tipton area. They had a lovely wedding and reception. I got really drunk,and remember afterwards driving home the wrong way down a one way street. They didn't go away on honeymoon but went straight back to their house. It was a joke afterwards as we found out Bill had taken his pyjamas in a paper bag to church, as he'd forgotten to leave them at their house.

Years had gone by since myself and my sisters had left Fraddon. Gloria had met Nicky who was in the Merchant navy. They decided to get married and did so in March 1961. I was very happy for them and travelled down to St Ives for the wedding. Nicky was from a large family so he had a lot of relatives there. On Gloria's side there was only myself, Aunty Leda and Aunty May. Dad and Olive didn't come. Gloria and Nicky paid for the wedding themselves as dad didn't want to put his hand in his pocket. Dad had never really been interested in us as kids and so the pattern continued.

My life rattled along as my friends and I continued going out on foursomes. Ron wanted us to get engaged, but I didn't feel I wanted to commit. I decided at 24 years my life was going nowhere at least nowhere I wanted. I couldn't see myself being a housewife and settling down. I wasn't ready and I wanted more from life. So I took the bull by the horns and decided once more to apply to join the WRNS in 1961.

2

I had to go to Burton-on-Trent for my entry exams, and a few weeks later I was informed I'd been accepted. This time I had decided to be a motor transport driver. I was given a date and joined a lot of other recruits at the training camp at Burghfield, Reading (HMS *Dauntless*) The first two weeks were the worst as we were put through our paces. Lots of lectures and lots of hard work. It was a wake up call.

So much to learn. Freedom taken, as we had to adjust to discipline and orders. Time being an important factor for duty. After a relaxed laid-back life before, it had all changed. I think it does so for the good, for self motivation and confidence.Two weeks was probation: if we found it wasn't our cup of tea, then it was time to bow out.

If you found it was still the kind of life you wanted to join, then that was the point to sign on for 4 years. I wasn't in any doubt - this is what I wanted. A bit scary at the same time, wondering what I'd let myself in for, or whether I'd even done the right thing. But nothing ventured nothing gained.

At this point we were issued with our uniform, which I did enjoy wearing, and felt smart. We were given a 24 hour pass which most of us took by going up to London in uniform, to see the sights. Then we had another short time of training before we each had a posting to various stations, to continue training in our various categories. There were three of us drafted to RNAS Culdrose as m/t drivers; others as stewards, writers etc were drafted elsewhere. Out of our group of trainees only about one girl decided to go home.The one thing about the WRNS is that it didn't come under the Naval discipline act and so a wren could walk out at any time, and not be brought back. The only thing I didn't like much was being on parades and marching. Still I was lucky enough in not *having* to, as I was required to drive personnel to these occasions and be on standby.

After we left Burghfield and before we joined Culdrose, we were given two weeks leave. So I spent it in Cornwall with Aunt Leda at Fraddon. In addition I took time to go to Stafford to see my friends and Ron. I was hoping Ron and I could still be friends, but he didn't want to know me, saying 'You've chosen the WRNS over me.' With hindsight I see that this was really true. So that was another piece of my life I was leaving behind.

One thing I left out about my training in Burghfield was that we had to experience tear gas. We were all given gas masks, told to enter a concrete bunker, the doors were closed and tear gas was pumped in. Our instructions were then to take the masks off inside and make a quick exit.It was horrendous, the gas was choking, my eyes were streaming and red, we all sat on the grass outside trying to get over the effects. It even clings to clothing, and so it was with us for a long time. Also that day we were instructed how to handle fires and had to take part in putting them out, on a big scale.

It was nerve racking at first at Culdrose but I gradually settled in and got on with the job. My life started to really take off. . . WOW!!!

I was always attracted to men in uniform so I was in my element. There were constant dates and parties, always something to do, and someone to do it with and at last I was enjoying my life.

During the second part of my training as a m/t driver at Culdrose, I met up with a guy from Scotland on the same course. We started going out on a regular basis. He came home to Fraddon with me a couple of times but I foolishly lent him money and never got it back - of course that was one thing the Navy tried to impress on our minds: never a lender nor a borrower be. One weekend when he came up to

Above: It's 1962 and I'm stationed with the WRNS at HMS Seahawk at Culdrose.

Left: 1963 recruiting tour with third officer Mallelu.

Fraddon for the weekend, I'd started to become bored with him and I began to drink alcohol in the house: I thought I might drink myself silly. After consuming a whole bottle of Johnnie Walker whiskey plus half a bottle of sherry, I passed out. It seemed to me that I never regained consciousness until the following day, but it turned out Aunt Leda had put me to bed and sat with me all through the night, as I was constantly throwing-up. I really believe I could have killed myself doing this with the drink, but at the time no one could reason with me. Aunt Leda never liked the man I'd met and after that weekend I finished with him.

I had now finished my second part of training and was told I would be staying at Culdrose (HMS *Seahawk*) as my first posting. I remember having only been at Culdrose for a couple of weeks as ship's company, when a squadron of sea venoms were sent to Ireland: two crashed and the crew killed - not a great start to my first station.There was always plenty to do socially on base: dances in the NAFFI or the PO's mess and cinema on camp sometimes. If anyone was interested in sport then there was plenty.I used to go into Helston sometimes with friends to the pub or shopping.

We had a varied roster rota for duty at the m/t section. Days, and then the evening duty which started at 5pm when we worked until the airfield closed flying for the night which was usually about 7 pm. Weekends we worked either a morning or an afternoon. Long weekends were from Friday to Tuesday lunchtimes every 6 weeks. That was really nice.

One evening when I was on duty, there was an aircraft still out, when we had the word the jet had gone down in the sea. So that night the airfield was open all night and I was on duty until 7am next morning. I was based in the control tower most of the night, driving personnel around. Quite a buzz of activity that night. Sadly to say the aircraft was recovered within a couple of days, but both the pilot and observer lost their lives. It's very sad when you know them personally, seeing them everyday.

My job was really good because I met up with a lot of different people, never knowing where I would be sent from one day to another.

So many places and different circumstances.Many times taking a crew from the armoury to pick up unidentified objects washed up on the beaches all around the coasts. At one time I had to drive the crew over to St Michael's Mount. A fisherman had picked up a suspect object in his fishing nets. It turned out nothing to be worried about as was each time. We had the tide to contend with, making sure we could drive back over the causeway.

While I was at Culdrose the station was put on 24 hour exercise simulating war. It was very interesting. I was responsible for driving a captain around all day, where ever he wanted to go on camp. He was such a nice man, and so concerned at one point - I hadn't been able to get anything to eat for quite sometime - that he went personally into the galley and had a parcel of food made up for me.

There was an old disused airfield about three miles away at Predannack which had been used during the war. This airfield was now being used for Culdrose gliding club and I joined up. To get airborne the tow hitch was attached to a truck which drove at speed up the runway to take up the slack. By the time the truck had reached the end of the runway we were airborne and could release the tow rope. It was a wonderful experience the silence of gliding, exhilarating. I decided I'd like to take the opportunity to fly but first had to go through the safety drills the same as the air crew, knowing what to do if the aircraft had to ditch during an emergency. Also how to use the ejector seat. I had to join pilots that were doing refresher drills in a static water tank. I was in a flight suit and had to inflate a dingy and crawl in, only to be tipped out to do it all again. I couldn't swim then and I still can't, but I didn't let that put me off.

My first flight was with an 809 squadron Mark 3 Gannet. The pilot and observer were in the front cockpit of the plane, while I was in the cockpit at the rear on my own with only radio for communication. It was wonderful as we flew right down over the isles of Scilly and back. We were airborne for about an hour.

A few of us wrens had been invited to a country club at the Lizard and it was there that I met Paul, a helicopter pilot, who came over and introduced himself. He was charming and good looking and I fell for him hook, line and sinker. After that evening he continued to phone the mess to take me out. We must have found all the lovely country pubs in Cornwall. He had a big old Wolseley car, quite tatty and a rattle trap, but it was comfy and it was fun. And he *was* fun to be with.

When I refer to the mess it was the wrens' quarters: buildings with long corridors with rooms off a corridor, sleeping up to 12 girls in a room. This is a situation where you have to be able to mix socially and get on with your colleagues as best as possible. We had mess inspections every week, everything had to be perfect - and floors highly polished. Not a speck of dust must be seen anywhere. After seeing each other for a few months, Paul was sent on a course to Ireland for a few weeks. He phoned me every day and it was so nice when he arrived back, and we could take up where we had left off. Early summer the next year, he invited me to spend two weeks' summer leave with him and invited me to meet his parents. They were staying at Wiveliscombe in North Devon, on holiday. As it turned out his father was a preacher and they were staying at the manse, having exchanged - with the preacher and his wife - their house in Diss, Norfolk for 2 weeks. His father must have been in his sixties and a very serious man, so Paul didn't 'turn after' his father. Paul was so crazy and fun loving: it was one round of parties and social events. One of his friends had a yacht moored at Coverack, and we used to go over some weekends sailing. One night we were invited on board for a meal. By the time we decided to leave to go back to camp it was late and getting dark. It seemed quite eerie going from yacht to shore, especially as the dingy was letting in water.

I used to pop up to Aunt Leda's sometimes when I had a long weekend, for a change. Some weekends I used to go down to stay with Gloria in St Ives: at this point she was married to Nicky but being in the Merchant Navy he was away abroad on trips for long lengths of time and she was on her own.

The next flight I was to take was with Paul at 805 squadron, in a dragonfly helicopter. He piloted the aircraft, with the observer beside him, and I sat behind Paul.This time we were again airborne for about an hour, but not having the speed of a jet, we just flew down over Cornwall to Lands End - a wonderful experience. I enjoyed every minute. It was nice seeing Paul in his working capacity. Mind you we were always bumping into one another during the course of the working day, either in the squadron or at Air traffic control.

When us wrens went out or ashore we had to sign out at the wrens' main Gate Office. If we wanted to stay out after midnight we had to get an S.O.P. (a sleeping out pass) and that would cover us for parties etc. Many of the girls including myself often didn't have an S.O.P. if it was a last minute invite, so we'd put a body in the bed (pillow) and made it look as if someone was there asleep, because the wren officer on duty often did a bed check after midnight with a torch. I used to creep in at the side gate and hope I didn't bump into her - I never did.

Dad was selling his car for another one, a little Morris Minor, so I decided to buy it from him as I thought being my dad he would see me right and I'd have a fair deal. Oh, but no. He did me down: I paid the going price because I thought it was a lovely car, but the gear box proved dodgy and the engine drank oil. Still I endured as I was now stuck with it, but it was a lovely little runabout and got me around a lot. By now Paul's car was a bit ancient and had seen better days, so we used mine a lot.

I was sent to R.N.A.S Yeovilton for a couple of weeks on a driving job. All the top brass were there as the Duke of Edinburgh was making an inspection of the base.

The highlight was a flypast of which the Duke took the salute. It started with all the old aircraft, the old string-back Tiger moth, the two in the aircraft stood up and saluted as they flew over the Duke. There were Spitfires, Lancasters, and on to the more up to date Buccaneers which followed.

By now dad and the family had moved to Darlington to look after his mum as she wasn't so good health -wise, and during another leave Paul travelled with me up to see dad. We stayed in bed and breakfast as they didn't have the room to put us up. That trip we got engaged, Paul proposing while we were up there. He bought me a beautiful diamond solitaire ring. It was a happy time. The following Christmas Paul and I went on leave to stay with his parents in Diss. They had a rambling old house (the manse) with a number of cats (who used to disappear into the depths of the house when they knew it was bedtime and they were due to be put out).

At RNAS Yeovilton on duty in 1963

His sister was away nursing so I never met her. New year's eve we went to a dance in Norwich and by the we left to come back to Diss, it was snowing hard. We ran into lots of drifts on the way home. It's a wonder we made it back at all, it was so cold and bleak. It' s such a flat county that gets a lot of the worse weather on that coast very little shelter. Months later, it was back to the day to day routine at Culdrose. Up to this point I haven't said, but Paul was very flirtatious, as I was to find out. One particular evening, I was on night duty. I had to drive down to the barrack area, outside of the wrens' quarters, when I saw Paul's car parked up. Curiosity got the better of me and I wandered over to check it out only to find a girl in the car with him. We had a furious row and I threw my ring back at him. Next day he kept ringing, but I refused take his calls. Eventually we did speak and he begged my forgiveness. We met up and did make up, and I took back his ring and wore it again, but it was always in the back of my mind that he could do it again. I didn't trust him after that, although I was still crazy about him. Long term I couldn't see any future for us, couldn't see how it could work with me and my doubts. Unknown to him I put in for a posting, and quite soon it came through. A posting back to Burghfield as ship's company in the all-female training base. He wanted me to re-consider and stay, but I was set on leaving, although we would still stay in touch. I think I was a bit hasty in taking that posting because being an all-female training base, it eventually got to me as I enjoyed male company a lot and here there was none. On leaving Culdrose I drove up by car to HMS *Dauntless* to start my posting in the winter of 1963. The weather had taken a turn for the worse after I left Culdrose, but I decided to carry on driving. It was snowing slightly but the further I travelled the worse it got. Instead of taking about 4 or 5 hrs for the journey, it took me more than 12 hours. It was late at night when I arrived and I was completely exhausted. It had snowed heavily, roads were blocked and iced up and it was a complete nightmare. Villagers came out to try and help the motorists pushing the cars. Over

Salisbury plain it was terribly bad. I've never had such a bad journey in all my life, especially as I was on my own. It was the start of the of the big freeze up. If I'd known it was going to be so bad I wouldn't have set out, but it was fine when I'd set out from Cornwall.

So now I had to settle in Burghfield and make the best of it. Thank goodness I had a car and could get out and about off duty.

I decided to put in for my killicks badge, (leading wren). I had to go back to Culdrose to do the course, being able to drive a 3 ton lorry - which I passed. It was nice going back and seeing everyone, but it's a fact you can never go back and expect things to be the same. I had moved on. Having passed the test I could now drive either the 3 ton lorry or the 13 seater bus into Reading to pick up the new recruits at the station. It was interesting seeing all the young hopefuls, some who took to the life while a small number went home.

Paul and I did meet up again, as he was sent on a course to RAF Old Sarum, Salisbury. I travelled to meet him for one weekend. It was still good, but I knew it could never be anything more.That time we paid a visit to Stonehenge - those were the days when you could walk all around the stones, not like now when it's all fenced off.

A recruiting job came up, to team up with a third officer wren, drive and travel with a large recruiting van. We were scheduled to visit various parts of the country, at venues that included all kinds of festivals and exhibitions. It meant we had a spot in these locations reserved through the navy, and we had to set up and show films. The idea was to interest girls in joining up. Also handing out literature and answering questions. This way we met a lot of nice people, and were often invited to the other exhibitors' stands for drinks. Third officer and myself were always booked into good hotels by the navy - all expenses paid.

One evening while we were in Birmingham my colleague was invited out by some friends she hadn't seen in a long time, who lived in the area - it was a good opportunity for her to meet up. This meant I was on my own and left to my own devices. After a meal in the hotel I decided to catch a bus and visit the cinema to see *Lawrence of Arabia* - which it turned out is quite a long movie - more than three and a half hours! When I came out it was very late, and I wasn't sure about the buses back to the hotel, so I decided to walk. This was a mistake, because I found I was being followed. I felt a bit scared but I didn't panic. I found the nearest telephone box and phoned for a taxi describing where I was, and explaining my situation. For safety's sake I stayed in the box until the taxi arrived, which it did promptly.

We were on the road touring for about 4 months which suited me fine. One of the places we visited was Wavertree in Liverpool. We saw the Cavern Club where the Beatles were discovered. Liverpool gave me the impression it was a lively, tough city. Daventry was another stop amongst many others. Then the tour was over.

Some friends of mine were friendly with some American aircrew stationed nearby and I was invited over with them to the base for drinks. It cut the boredom of the all female company, they were a nice crowd and we had some good nights out.

Then Ann a friend of mine introduced me to Bob and Steve they were aircrew stationed at RAF Abingdon a base nearby. Bob and Ann were going out, so we used to make up a foursome. As time went on, Ann and Bob split up. Bob and I became attracted to one another, and he asked me out. Steve and I hadn't been really compatible. With Bob and I used to go over to Oxford quite a lot for walks by the river. Also a favourite place was Henley-on-Thames. We had only been going out a short time when he had a posting to RAF Linton-on-Ouse, in Yorkshire. We kept our friendship going by writing and he would phone me. One weekend when he came down to Reading, he proposed to me and bought a sapphire and diamond ring. I accepted and invited him to come with me on summer leave to Cornwall where he could meet my family, Aunt Leda, and Gloria in St Ives.

We had a great holiday and he then invited me to meet his parents in Lincoln. He wanted us to get a special licence and get married right away as he didn't want to wait. I asked, 'What's the hurry?' I wanted to finish my time in the WRNS of which there was a year yet to run. I used to join him sometimes in York, have bed and breakfast and then enjoy social nights at the RAF base. I loved York especially the quaintness of the *Shambles* and the beautiful cathedral. He was a keen rower and part of a crew that went out on the Ouse at weekends. Often at the weekends, he would be on the river, and I would be waiting in the clubhouse with his friends in the bar. I was enjoying life, and was quite infatuated with Bob.

Time was ticking by, when suddenly events took a nasty turn. It was now summer and my camp had been approached by a prowler. We slept in individual cabins in long wooden huts. Whoever it was would tap on a girl's window and then run away. One day we were sunbathing outside the hut and saw a man running like mad down the field behind the camp. We joked and said 'there goes our prowler' but funnily enough, it turned out it actually was. The next moment a fire engine came tearing into camp, and up to the sick bay where the man had set a fire through one of the open windows. The police also arrived to investigate. These events didn't bother myself nor any of the other girls, who thought it was a bit pathetic, and things would settle down. When it came to summer leave I decided to take mine at a later date, to fit in with plans I'd made. So I stayed behind as skeleton crew - someone had to stay on camp - enough to keep the place open. It was quite nice really just a few of us so relaxed from duty. So there was only myself and three other girls in the long sleeping block. One night I was awakened by a slight noise at the window. I sat up and listened, realising someone was trying to break in. There was a small push out top window which I always left open, with a large window below, which was shut. For a moment I sat up in bed as a chill went right through me and I froze, unable to move. I let out a scream, and in that instant it must have un-nerved him and stopped him in his tracks. I rushed out into the corridors the other doors opened and the girls rushed out to see what all the commotion was all about. I remember I was shaking like a leaf. I dialled the camp switchboard and they in turn contacted the police. They came within minutes, with a police dog.

Before the police arrived,with the company of another girl I went back to my cabin.Whoever it was, had actually opened the big window and the curtains were blowing. If I hadn't woken when I did, I hate to think what might have happened. The police did a search with the dog, but whoever it was had gotten away. Next morning you could see where the intruder had stood, the grass was flattened and there were boot scratch marks up the side of the cabin where he'd climbed up.

After that incident however hot it was, I slept with my windows closed, my lights on, and a stick under my pillow. I didn't ever feel safe there at night again. I put in for a posting to get away as my nerves were on edge. Under the circumstances I was given one almost immediately to HMS *Fulmar* RNAS Lossiemouth in Scotland. I was delighted to have this posting especially as it was in Scotland, and new places to see. I drove up by car, giving myself plenty of time, days in fact stopping at various places for bed and breakfast and sightseeing. Pitlochry, Gretna Green, Aviemore - very beautiful country especially the highlands.

And so I began the last part of my four years at Lossiemouth and settled in very well though I had to get used to the very cold weather. The camp was situated about one mile away from the fishing village of Lossiemouth. The town of Elgin was the nearest place for shopping. With Marjorie, a friend of mine from the mess, I used to go into Elgin most Saturdays for shopping, cream tea, cinema, and then fish and chips before returning to camp. Our cabin housed about five of us again in wooden huts. We had an old

We heard on the grapevine that Prince Charles was coming from Gordonstoun (where he was at school) to Lossiemouth, so we made a quick dash up to the harbour to get a glimpse of him. He was going out to board the Royal Yacht *Britannia*, which was anchored in the bay. The harbour was crowded as a dirty old Land Rover pulled up and out jumped Prince Charles. He was quite young at the time. In a split second he was taken out by motor launch. I was surprised that the yacht wasnt as big as I'd expected.

I decided I should pick myself up and get on with things, snap out of my depression, so I put in for another flight. I had to go through all the safety drills again. The day came for the flight, it was a pilot and a hunter hawk jet from the squadron I was attached to. The lads who worked on the engines started pulling my leg by saying, 'I wouldn't fly if I were you, we work on those engines!' I sat alongside the pilot this time for the hour-long flight. We took the route over Inverness, down over Loch Ness and over Ben Nevis, Obern, across the Isle of Skye going north before coming back to Lossiemouth. This was the best of all flights, because at one point the pilot said, 'Take over the joystick and see how it feels to manoeuvre the plane.' I didn't want that flight to end and can't express how it made the adrenalin flow.

One day my duty was to pick up the crew of a Vulcan V Bomber that had just flown in and take them to the Officers Mess. They were a bunch of nice guys, five of them, and were due to fly out the next day. I once again had to pick them up and bring them over to the squadron. All of them were joking and laughing. I stood outside the hanger and watched as they took off, the great plane roaring up into the sky. A short time later we heard the devastating news, that something had gone wrong, they had crashed and were all killed. It made me feel cold.

I used to go up to the NAFFI club a lot socially, there was usually a group of us get together round a table for drinks when it was dance night.

1965: At the Gliding club which I joined at RNAS Fulmar Lossiemouth.

I starting dating Mick, a driver on the fire crew, a nice guy who was engaged to a girl in Civvy Street, so it was nothing serious. My time was coming to an end in the Navy and it was strange to feel I was going to be 'free'.

When the time came I was tearful, and it was a wrench to leave so many good friends. Unless you've been in the services it's difficult to know what I mean. It's like a compact family with its own, different sense of humour. A civilian may not understand. Of course there were ups and downs, but I did enjoy those four years.

Coming out I was at a loss. It seemed Civvy Street was so dull, so uneventful and boring. I would have stayed and signed on again but for the fact that I was now 28 years old, and the best years to be in the services is in your early twenties. Service life gives you a wonderful life, travel, sport, and most of all the comradeship of a big family.

Aunt Leda was glad to welcome me back to Cornwall, but I had to decide what to do for the future and a job. I felt very unsettled and undecided. So I didn't rush into anything, I decided to go down to St Ives to see Gloria and my little niece and nephew, Karen and Peter, and just chill out for a while.

3

It was 1966 and I had different ideas of a job, none of which materialized. Then, much to Aunt Leda's horror I decided to write to an agency in *The Lady* magazine and apply for a job as a mother's aid/ children's nanny in America. As I have previously said we have family who had emigrated to California. I wrote to them and told them of my plans and shortly the Agency put me in touch with a family in Los Angeles. I thought it sounded just the job for me and decided to go ahead with it.

Firstly I had to apply for a working visa, so I had to go to the American Embassy in London for an interview which took all day. While I was waiting for my visa to materialise which took a few weeks, I decided I'd like to meet up again with Bill and Jean in Tipton, Staffs. I stayed with them and got a temporary job for a bit of pocket money, in the office of an iron foundry.

Looking back, I was so glad I'd broke away from Stafford years ago. I knew then that at that time I would have been bored being married, and living there. I always needed new challenges whereas Jean, on the other hand, was happy and settled, although unfortunately she had developed heart problems, since I last saw her.

At last my visa arrived. Aunt Leda was convinced she would never see me again, and was quite upset at me going. The agency had taken care of all my job details and flight arrangements. Agency rules said that the family had to initially pay for my flight, and then would take a percentage out of my wages until the flight was paid.

Preparing for my trip to LA in the run up I had sent on in advance a trunk and a suitcase by sea. My thoughts were to stay for a long time, and even included in the trunk an iron! Something I wouldn't dream of taking now. I remember the day I left Fraddon I'd booked a taxi to take me to St Austell station to catch the London train. Aunt Leda came to wave me off, it must have been awful for her, now thinking back. She was smiling and put on a brave face and wished me well.

But I was told afterwards her heart was breaking because she thought she'd never see me again. Youngsters never see these things. That day I felt numb, no feelings of fear nor excitement. I travelled up to London the day before my flight, and had bed and breakfast in London. I caught a coach from Victoria to Heathrow the following morning.

In the mid-1960s there was no travelling in casual clothes, I wore a very smart linen two piece suit and high heels, which I'd bought for the occasion. I always liked to have a smart fashionable appearance. As luck might have it the girl I sat next to me on the flight was from St Columb Minor (my home territory, near Newquay). She was travelling out also to Los Angeles from the same agency as myself. She was travelling to the suburb of Van Nuys,which is north of LA. We had a stop over for a couple of hours in New York for refueling and when we stepped out of the aircraft to enter the rest area, the heat just hit us. After the cold September rain that we'd left behind in London this was quite a shock.

Later we re-boarded the aircraft and had another stop over in San Francisco where we changed from our BOAC flight to Western Airlines for the connection to Los Angeles. San Francisco airport was choc-a-block with service men all waiting to be flown out to Viet Nam. I was so tired when I finally arrived at L. A. Airport - it had been so many long hours since we left London. My hosts Dr. and Mrs. Redlar were there to meet me and to drive me to their home.

It was a lovely, warm scented evening with the sound of crickets: I felt as though I was in another world. The journey in their car had taken about 45 minutes to their home in Kenter Canyon in the suburbs of Brentwood. Brentwood, Westwood, and Hollywood all adjoin one another. It was so late at night and I was glad to get to bed.

Next morning I met all the family and the little children I was to look after. Jill was 4 years old, Bonnie was 2, and Kenny was just four weeks old. There was a live-in nurse there taking care of Kenny, but she left a couple of weeks of my arriving. Then they were in my sole care. They were very spoilt, and I had my work cut out with them.

The family had quite a lovely house, well spread out with large bungalow-style rooms. My en-suite room was the smallest. At the back of the house was a large garden patio with lemon and orange trees.Everything spoke money, as it was in a wealthy area. Dr Redlar was a dentist and had his practice in Beverly Hills where a number of his patients were movie stars, and other well known people. While I was living with them, he kindly took care of my teeth. Mrs Redlar was a chairwoman of various organisations, and very often had

Brentwood Los Angeles 1966. I've arrived here as Nanny/ Mother's help to look after these little ones.

women around to the house for meetings and coffee mornings. Once she appeared on TV giving a speech; always well-dressed and made up, Mrs. Redlar never did anything in the house apart from the cooking and even then her cooking was rather basic, amounting as it almost always did to meat loaf. I found, therefore, that I was working quite hard, doing all the housework, and looking after three children. It was like being married but without the pleasure.

Luckily for me there was an English girl living with the next door family. Her situation was different from mine, as she had been there for years looking after the children who had now grown up. She was more of a companion to them now, as their parents were professional people. Her name was Shirley and she was good company. Having use of the family's car, we could visit places. My working arrangements were from 8.00 am until the children went to bed. Days off on Wednesdays and every other Sunday. Besides my other duties I was expected to baby-sit most nights when they went out.

As soon as I arrived I felt they left me to it. I was looking forward to at least a small amount of free time once the children had gone bed but this turned out not to be the case. It seemed to me that I was rather taken for granted as unfortunately the previous girl had been quite happy to work evenings as well because she never wanted to go out. Being so far from home I never felt strong enough to protest. The first time I'd made arrangements to go out I was told to cancel as they were going out instead. So right from the start things were not perfect. When I used to go next door to see Shirley on the evenings I *could* get out I used to say it was like being let out of prison.

Shirley and I joined a group to learn to play guitar, and I arranged to borrow an instrument as I didn't have my own.

The Redlars were a Jewish family and celebrated Hanukkah, so that was all new to me with the lighting of the candles. Our property didn't have a swimming pool, but Shirley and I were sometimes invited over to a neighbours, to swim in their outdoor heated pool which was lovely. All the people in our drive seemed connected in some way either to the Hi-Fi business or to the owners of Max Factor. The weather was ideal: it was lovely to have the sun every day, and I now had a lovely tan whereas before, when I first arrived, I was lily white. It made a change if it rained, which wasn't very often. When it did rain it would rain torrents for days, and you would think it was never going to stop.

I'd written to my folks in San Bernardino, and a few weeks after I arrived, one of their family - Richard, Mom Coles' son - came to pick me up and take me over there for a Thanksgiving meal. It was so nice meeting them for the first time. Mom Cole (May) was about 82 years old and was the daughter of my great grandfather's brother who had emigrated there many years ago, as I said earlier. Mom's daughter Alma was head teacher at the high school in San Bernardino.

Walter, mom's son-in-law was a scientist with the government. He could never discuss his work, as it was all top secret stuff, but said we would be in awe if we knew what was going on. They had three daughters and a beautiful home with a swimming pool. It was just like being at the movies, none of it seemed real to me. I was in a higher state of living than I'd ever been used to, out of this world. Her son Richard was involved with high tech work, an inventor of sorts, he was involved with the creation of the making and technology of the series of 'Thunder Birds' on TV. Arthur was another son, who came to the thanksgiving dinner with his wife Aileen. So you can imagine it was quite a big get together.

The girl I'd travelled on the plane with to L A - we never met up again as there was quite a distance between Brentwood and Van Nuys - but we often spoke on the phone. Sometimes I worked my time off, to get extra time to go away for a weekend now and then. My idea was to make the most of my stay over there, to see as much of the area and country as I could. One weekend Shirley and I flew up to San Francisco . What a magical city I found it to be.

Like the song:

Above: Thanksgiving dinner, 1966, with the Cole family at San Bernadino. May Cole (third from the left on the sofa) is the daughter of Richard White. I am sat at the back on the right.

The loveliness of Paris seems somehow sadly gay
The glory that was Rome is of another day

'I Left My Heart in San Fransisco', that applies to me. It was the middle of the 1960s and the time of hippies, flower power and the beginning of smoking cannabis [peace man!) openly. We saw a lot of that: gentle people, with flowers in their hair, all rather 'laid back', and very happy.We visited all the tourist spots, Knob Hill where all the fashionable hotels are, right at the top of the hill which have been featured in many films. Shirley and I took ourselves in one and made our way up to the restaurant on the top floor. The view was breathtaking being so high it felt like the floor was moving. You had a sense of not being able to stand still (and, no, we hadn't had any alcohol to drink!). Then it was Coit

Tower and Fisherman's Wharf where there were so many fish restaurants, and where, outside on the wharf were the open take-away restaurants where all the fish is cooked in front of you. The smell of the fish was quite overpowering. Any kind of fish you wanted was there.

Golden Gate park was so beautiful the grounds were laid out so well, including the Chinese gardens where the Magnolia Trees were all out in blossom. Chinatown was interesting, with all their wares in the shop windows, especially the shops selling food and where the chickens looked as though they had been put through a mangle, as they were flat. We walked until we thought our legs would drop off, though we also used the trams as they were so cheap to jump on and off - just a few cents. We took a trip over to Sausalito harbour, which was over the Golden Gate Bridge. The bridge itself is not golden, but a rusty red. I loved Sausalito with all its luxury yachts, quite a pretty harbour. And of course we saw Alcatraz island, as we took a boat trip in the bay.

Another day that weekend we took a trip up to see the Giant Redwoods - really something - the massive heights of those trees, were amazing. The hotel we stayed in was in Union Square the centre of the city, so as you can imagine it was an ideal location for us. As it happened it was also used by the airline crews for stop overs. The flight up that weekend was rough, and we ran into a very bad storm and lightning - we were bucked about quite a bit.

Poor Shirley was quite ill and had to reach for her sick bag. In the window seat by us was a nun. When the storm began, she started praying, so that didn't do much for our confidence.The runway we came in on ran parallel with the stretch of water of the bay on our right which was different from most airports.

The flight back was a different story, very calm and enjoyable. As it was a night flight, the lights of L A when we were coming in to land were quite magical and something I'll never forget.

Golden Gate Bridge from the Sausolito side.

While I was living with the Redlars my cousin wrote and told me he was getting married. I couldnt get back for the wedding, so he sent me photographs and a box of wedding cake. I was looking forward to tasting the cake, when behind my back, Bonnie had got hold of the box and ate the lot.I wasnt very happy.

She was quite a handful, another time she got up on the table and poured a jug of milk into the fish tank. Changing the water in the fish tank was something I hated doing at the best of times. I had to rescue those fish quickly, amazingly they all survived.

Shirley was taking her charge (Cookie) to see a show in the San Fernando Valley and I was invited to go with them. It was the first time that I'd seen a stage in the centre (I think actors call it 'in the round') with the audience all around, and catwalks for audience participation. Shirley had been with her hosts for years looking after the children while they were growing up so now they regarded her as one of the family. She was allowed to take the car anytime to go anywhere, and was telling me of the time she went to a Christmas carol service and found herself sitting next to Pat Boone. She very often used to see some movie star or other while she was out.

Andy Williams was a favourite singer of mine and I applied for tickets to one of his shows, but was told there was an 18 month waiting list - needless to say I never did get to see him.

Maxine, the girl who was my predecessor, was still living in L. A. after her year with at the Redlars as she had decided to stay on in the city and get another job. She kept in touch with Shirley who she'd also been friendly with, and one day we all got together and drove down to Disneyland. My impression of Disney was magic and I vowed I would go back one day and see it all again.

On another day's leave I decided to take off on a tour bus to Universal Studios in Hollywood. Then it was not a made up set, but the real studios where the films were shot. I saw Robert Wagner who looked even better in real life than on screen. Alfred Hitchcock didn't have a normal key to his trailer, but instead had a safe dial to open his door - something different, I suppose. Also I was taken through Lana Turner's dressing rooms, as she wasn't on set that day.

I very often on my days off would catch a bus down to Santa Monica to shop or have time on the beach. The sand was so hot you could burn your feet. The Esplanade above the beach is where a lot of films are shot, plus the well known Santa Monica pier.

Shirley and I went to Malibu one day hoping to see the surf, but were disappointed because it was flat. Still we had a nice meal in a restaurant on the pier, where all the walls were covered with film stars' pictures past and present. Shirley and I went for a meal one evening in Westwood, in a little restaurant where the 'The Mammas and The Pappas' were discovered. Typical western country-style restaurant with check tablecloths and the waiting staff in cowboy and cowgirl outfits.

Other days we visited Hollywood, and the Chinese Grauman's Theatre (now called TCL Chinese Theatre) where all the famous foot and handprints are on the pavements. I used to catch the bus to Hollywood on my own sometimes to look around the shops - it was very nice to see but very expensive. Having to use public transport when I went out alone there was a drawback: the bus stop was a long way from where I lived. Needless to say you really need a car for getting around over there. The walk from the house in Kenter Canyon to the bus on Wiltshire Boulevard took me about 20 mins. One evening when I came back from Santa Monica and got off the bus, I noticed a group of about a dozen black guys blocking the pavement - not deliberately, in fact they were all just chatting. Still, there was no-one else around, it was dark, and I felt very nervous, but I thought 'I've got to pass them somehow to get home, and not show my fear'. So I did. I held my head high and didn't look at them - just walked straight past, although I was shaking. It was the time of the Civil Rights Marches and there had been racial tension in the suburbs of the city, in Watts, just before I arrived. The predominantly black area of Watts had been on national news with riots and looting of shops.

On another of my days off I was walking up from Wiltshire Boulevard when I caught some dirt in my eye from a passing car. I couldn't seem to clear it even when I got home. That evening my eye was in quite a state. Mrs Redlar was quite unperturbed and thought I was fussing. I went next door to visit Shirley and both her and her family became concerned. Shirley drove me to UCLA hospital, in Westwood to get a doctor to look at it. It appeared I had some grit lodged, and had scratched my cornea. So after the hospital washed it and put drops in, I had to wear an eye patch for 24 hours. I had terrible headaches, but Mrs Redlar still expected me to do my work, which I skipped over. They were a rather self-centred couple.

One weekend I quite enjoyed was when Arthur (Mom Coles' son) and his wife Aileen, picked me up and took me to spend the weekend with them in their cabin in the mountains of San Bernardino. It was so cold at night and I was glad of the electric blanket. In the mornings I was awakened by the squirrels racing across the roof. They were quite tame really, in the fact we used to feed them peanut butter off a spoon. It was so quiet and peaceful and the air so fresh, away from the smog of the city. In L A when you looked down over the city from the Santa Monica hills, you could see the haze, just like a blanket-covering. When you were down in the city especially on a very hot day your eyes would sting and smart. Anyway Arthur and Aileen were both religious people and would pray during the last meal before we left to go home, and ask God to take hold of the steering wheel and guide our car safely down the mountain roads.

Below: Myself, Arthur and Aileen Cole at their cabin in the San Bernardino mountains.

The views were wonderful over the valley and we stopped off to admire the view of Lake Arrowhead - a popular place where people visited to fish and sail. Then it was down and back onto the freeway ready to join the rat race.

They were very good to me and liked showing off their country, because another time they took me on a trip into the desert to Palm Springs to take a cable car ride up into the mountains. That was really something: there were racoons running all over the place. We spent a few hours walking around and having lunch.

I've been so lucky with all these experiences in my life. Sometimes you just have to go out and get the things you want: they don't come to you easily and life is what you make it.

Although my job was quite hard and at times I felt so homesick for England, I wanted to see and do as much as I could with my time there. So another weekend I took off again, on my own. With nothing pre-booked, I caught a bus down to Long Beach and checked out the flights to Catalina Island, and paid for a seat on a sea plane. Everything was so relaxed over there that when I was safely on board I asked if I could sit in the cockpit with the pilot. I said I was ex British-Navy and loved flying. I couldn't believe my luck when I was told, 'Yes'!

That, again was really something. Taking off from the sea, with a cockpit view, rather than back with the passengers, the windscreen wipers working like mad as the spray came up and we took off. It seemed a rattley old aircraft as though it might fall to bits but the weather was good and we had a good flight over. By boat it takes about 2 hours, but by sea-plane about 45 minutes. Soon we were at Santa Catalina Island and landed on the sea in Avalon harbour, disembarking at the pier.

This was the bay where some years later in 1981 the movie star Natalie Wood would drown while on a yacht with her husband Robert Wagner. At the time she was in the middle

The Bay of Avalon, Catalina Island.

of making her last film *Brainstorm* and the circumstances of her death have always been mired in controversy.

On arriving on the island I had to find somewhere to stay, so I checked the seafront motels, and booked into a very nice one. It was lovely at night to hear the surf lapping on the beach just a few steps across the road. Next day I took a coach tour of the island and met up with some nice people. We visited a ranch where they bred Arabian horses, then went on to see wild buffalo which roam the plains of the island. Apparently they were taken there some years previous for a movie and were never shipped back. A lot of movies are shot on Catalina and around the jetty.

I became friendly with a guy that was on the tour: Ed, who was an ex-pilot back from serving his time in Vietnam. He had a family on the island and took me to meet them. We spent an hour or so there, sipping cool drinks and watching the humming birds in the garden. I was amazed how small those little birds are. When the weekend came to an end Ed and I travelled back by seaplane together. He had his car parked in Long Beach and kindly offered me a lift back to L.A. After that meeting we went out a couple of times, usually over to Hollywood for evenings out.

Time went on and I got increasingly discontented with things at the Redlars, made worse by the fact that I was also very homesick. My contract was up so I called it a day with them. I'd paid my outbound airfare back and decided to leave. I could have found something else but I didn't want to stay in the country any longer. If I did, I felt I would have started putting down roots and then it would have been increasingly difficult to move back home. I knew the home for me was England. Before I left California my folks invited me to spend some time over with them in San Bernardino, and Ed kindly offered to drive me over.

Anyway the day came for me to leave, I left San Bernardino on the El Capitan train. The trains were so clean and comfortable, reclining seats and plenty of pillows for long journeys. I'd bought a ticket to New York, but decided to make a stop-over on the way. This I did at a place called Flagstone, where I caught a coach to the Grand Canyon.

I booked in for a couple of nights at the Bright Angel Lodge. Next day I did a sightseeing tour along the rim of the canyon. It's a place I'd always wanted to go.

The canyon itself is fantastic, from morning to night the colours change continually over the canyon, as the sun moves about, morning from red, to the evening blue.

Every moment was a different colour. There was a large vast patio area at the back of the lodge overlooking the rim. A whole family of chipmunks were living just over the rim, and it was lovely to watch them scurrying around oblivious

The Grand Canyon, Arizona.

to everyone. The guests were entertained at times during the day, on the patio by red Indians dancing in full costume, rain dancing etc, quite colourful. I had an 8mm cine camera all these times with me and captured it all. Evenings there would be choirs of young people in evening dress singing out on the patio. There were a number of English people staying there. I had dinner one evening with a young guy from Lebanon, who was also travelling alone. There were mule trips down into the canyon. I didn't fancy that myself as I heard various people saying it was rather hard on the bottom. The mule train went down one day, stayed overnight in the canyon and came up the next day.They were told to be aware of rattle-snakes - not my cup of tea.

I took about three or four days to journey from one coast to the other having stopped off. I didn't want to fly home yet as it was too quick, I wanted to see a bit of the country first. I quite enjoyed the train. It had an observation car, where you could go up and take in all the views. The train follows the famous 'Route 66' across country.

I had to change at Central station in Chicago, to go on to New York. The 'redcaps' (porters) were very helpful with directions and helping with my luggage.

The journey from Chicago to New York wasn't so luxurious, just a normal train as it was a shorter journey. I could have had a sleeper, but had to be careful about money as my funds were limited. I arrived in New York in the morning, and had all day in the city before my flight home in the evening. I'd planned it that way. Because I had my luggage to consider and didn't want to drag it around with me I found a locker, though in what building, now, I can't remember. Then I took yellow cabs around the city, firstly to the Empire State Building. It consists of 106 floors, and I took the lift up to the observation floor on the 102 floor. The lifts consisted of one going halfway, then transfering to another and going the rest of the way up. The views were fantastic over the whole city and looking down, the traffic looked like ants. I took loads of 8mm cine film, which is now gathering dust in the loft.

Later I took to the water in a boat trip all around the bay, including the Statue of Liberty, Ellis Island, Manhattan, Brooklyn Bridge and so on. Travel is so much better than books can ever be.

The day was ticking by, so I went back to pick up my luggage, before catching another cab to Kennedy Airport for my evening flight home to London. This time I used a Pan AM flight. By now my money was really running out and I had just budgeted enough to buy a train ticket from Paddington, home to Cornwall and Aunt Leda's.

My return to England was eye-opening: back to dirty, smutty, steam trains, and back to the rain and the cold again, although it was summer. I couldn't get warm after California's heat. I wore jumpers but still I shivered. I'd been used to going barefoot a lot of the time over there, even down the road, so it felt awful to get back into shoes. Of course, it was lovely to see my family again and I was really glad to be home. America is a lovely country and fine for a holiday but for me it was not somewhere I could live permanently. It was so nice catching up with my sister Gloria and her two little ones, Peter and Karen, in St Ives. Nicky, my brother-in-law, still with the Merchant Navy was overseas on a trip.

Not having a car, and little money I'd decided to hitch hike down to St.Ives, something I'd never done before, and wouldn't do again.

At one point I went to stay with Uncle Eddie and Aunty May in Plympton for a few days as they'd invited me to stay any time I wanted. It was nice catching up on shopping in Plymouth. I thought about getting a job and a flat in Plymouth, but it didn't materialize as I was too comfortable at Aunt Leda's.

I very soon got myself a job in Newquay, as a shop assistant in Dingles which was later taken over by the House of Frazer, the main store being in Plymouth. In fact I had the chance to work at the Plymouth branch, in the china department, but decided to stay at Newquay on the hosiery and handbag floor. I quite enjoyed the job apart from one member of staff who took a dislike to me and at times made life very difficult for me hoping, i believe, that I would leave. I never give in to bullying and if anyone has to go, it's not going to be me. The senior person on my department left, and I took over her job, which included ordering for our shop what we needed from Plymouth. Sometimes I had to travel up to the main store to pick out a new stock of handbags.

4

During the time after I had returned home from America, Aunt Leda had become sick and had to go into Truro hospital for a gallstones operation and around the same time the doctors discovered she had breast cancer and needed a breast removed. They decided to do both operations under the same anaesthetic as she needed them both doing urgently. Leda was blighted with health problems all her life, and now this: the poor woman was rarely out of pain.

She went through the process of treatment bravely, and told everyone she was cured, which was far from the truth.The treatment was just holding it back. We never knew whether or not she really knew the truth and I suspect she didn't. Doctors were not so forthright then as they are now. However Aunt Leda did well for many years after all this.

Right out of the blue one day outside the railway station in Newquay, a young guy stopped me for directions. He had just parked is car and was a stranger to the town having just driven down for the day from Buckland Brewer in North Devon. We got chatting and he seemed so nice. He asked if I'd like to join him for a drink, which I accepted. That young guy was Donald (Don as I would call him) and cupid had sprung his arrow. We had an immediate attraction to one another and agreed we'd like to see each other again. Aunt Leda didn't have the luxury of a phone at home, and neither did Don's family, so we made arrangements to use the public phone boxes in our respective villages. He used to come down some weekends or I would go up to his place. He was living at home with his mum and dad as he had just returned from Germany where he had been with the British army having served 12 years. One Sunday when he came down as usual, having always to borrow his dad's car, we drove into Newquay for the day and decided at one point to drive up onto the cliff tops at Pentire for some quiet time to talk and get to know each other a bit more. It was a beautiful afternoon and lovely looking over the sea. As the day wore on, and we decided it was time to leave, Don tried to reverse the car. However it wouldn't go back up and he couldn't get a grip, and it kept slipping further and further down the cliff. Don tried putting the rubber mats under the back wheels but to no avail. It came to the point where it was in sheer danger and he took off to find a garage who then had the task of putting a tow rope on, and pulling it back from the cliff face.

It was quite scary really, especially as it was his father's car, but he never told him, otherwise he probably wouldn't have been allowed to borrow it again.

Don and I met in May 1969; were engaged in June and married in September. One weekend while I was at his home he'd asked me to marry him, and I said 'Yes'. I knew he was the one for me, and that this was the real thing. I was determined now that it was time for me to settled down, so I had no intentions of letting him go. Anyway at 32 years and him 34 years it was the ideal time. We were both ready. He had been married and divorced years previous. We decided we would get married in September so it was a whirlwind four months.

We went down to St Ives so he could meet dad, but it wasn't an ideal meeting. I finished up in tears - dad's usual effect. So after that I decided I wasn't going to ask him to give me away, instead I asked Uncle Eddie and he was pleased to do it.

Aunt Leda found it difficult getting workmen to do jobs for her. She had a big garden at the back, which grandpa used to look after when he was alive, but now it was going to rack and ruin; overgrown to say the least. I thought as I was young fit and healthy I would try to help.We got in someone with a mechanical digger and uprooted all the fruit bushes. Then it was my turn, I dug and turned up all the soil picking out all the heavy stones and carrying them away. I borrowed a heavy concrete roller from a neighbour to roll the soil nice and flat to seed it in grass. It would make life a bit easier for her. Mind you it was heavier work than I expected and it resulted in me slipping a disc. I woke one morning and couldn't move I was in so much pain. My doctor was useless to say the least, didn't have a clue, just gave me painkillers, and wouldn't consider an X-ray. My back problems was then to continue on and off for the rest of my life. Looking back I wish I hadn't done that job.

There were weekends Don and I couldn't meet up because of my back pains. Anyway eventually I got sorted and the pain went away,so we could look forward to getting married. We decided on the date of 6th September 1969. This time around I told Don I wasn't bothered about an engagement ring as neither of us had very much money, and the wedding ring was more important.

I left my job in the shop a week before so I could make all the arrangements. The day I left the shop, unknown to me, the girls had tied a lot of tin cans to the back bumper of the car. I'd arranged to give a girl a lift home, so it must have looked funny as I drove through Newquay with all the tin cans clattering and everyone looking. I had paid for the wedding reception in Fraddon village hall, out of my limited funds. Once again dad hadn't offered, so I had to budget very carefully.

Don was going to pay for the honeymoon, though he too had little funds. We had booked a week in Torquay.

Weddings and wedding dresses were so much affordable in those days. I bought a beautiful white dress that had a fitting bodice of broderie anglaise lace, long sleeves, a mandarin collar and a train. I'd been to Plymouth and bought it off the peg. I had my hair washed and set in the little village hairdressers the day before the wedding, and went down the morning of the wedding to have it combed out. How things have changed now. Car-wise I had by now bought a little Morris Minor, that Don and I were going to go away in. My next door neighbour let me park it in her garage, secretly, as I knew what would happen: things would have been tied to it and sprayed 'just married' and what-have-you on the back. So it stayed in there until we were ready to leave.

The day of the wedding was so warm and sunny - it just couldn't have been better. The wedding and reception went like a dream and I just floated through the day - the most wonderful day of my life. Here I was, married to the most wonderful man in the world, whom I adored and loved very much. At last I had found my soul mate. Most of the guests were on Don's side. He had a brother and five sisters, plus their families and his mum and dad. My family was smaller only having two sisters. Barbara was my bridesmaid, Gloria and her two children Peter and Karen. Nicky was away at sea. There was Uncle Eddie who gave me away, Aunt Leda and a few friends of mine. Dad didn't come to the wedding although he was invited. He drove my sisters up to Fraddon to be at my wedding then he waited in the pub until they were ready to go back to St Ives. After the reception we left for the honeymoon, but not before we rang Don's sister Wendy who was in hospital and hadn't been able to come. She had given birth to a son just two days before. Again we had to use the public telephone box in the village. We both crammed in, me in my wedding dress, and had a chat with her before we went back to the house to change. Before leaving the village I put my wedding bouquet on my mother's grave. We drove to Torquay and checked into our hotel. Two people very much in love.

We intended staying a week, but fate had decided otherwise.

Next day we visited Cockington village - a very pretty place - and had a drink in the pub. The following day we decided to go to the model village at Babbacombe. It was beautiful weather and Don had slung his coat over his shoulder, because it was so warm. On arriving there he went to get his wallet out, and I saw by the look of horror on his face, that it had gone. Either it had dropped out or it had been stolen. I paid the entrance fee, and we went in but neither of us felt very happy. He had only been carrying cash. Neither of us had a bank account so didn't have cards nor a cheque book. The decision had to be made,and we had to cut short our honeymoon. I had just enough money to pay for the hotel weekend and the petrol back.

We made the best of a bad thing, and thinking back we didn't really worry too much about it. We could have got married at a later date and saved a bit but we felt we'd be wasting time not being together. We came back via Widecombe-in-the-Moor and, as it happened to our advantage, it was Widecombe Fair, with Uncle Tom Cobley and all! The festival was opened by the singer Kathy Kirby.

The flat we were going to rent in Instow wouldn't be ready for a few days, so we had to spend the rest of the week at his mum and dad's, which was very kind of them but less than ideal. His mum didn't have a spare double bed, so she put two singles together - the only thing was, one was slightly higher than the other, and the bed springs creaked like mad so we hardly dare move.

The flat was on a six month's lease until March 1970, so it did us for the time, and we could look around for something more permanent. Don was working for a wine merchants, driving a delivery lorry with beer for pubs. When he had a few longer trips down to Crackington Haven and Bude, I used to go with him. This was until one day he had a disagreement with his boss and walked out. So he was on the dole for a while chasing jobs. I had a couple of jobs in shops in Bideford one after another but couldn't settle. Don then got himself a short term job at Appledore Shipbuilders where buildings were being constructed. Don's job was to accompany the surveyor sizing up the site to build. He found it so boring just standing around holding the poles for measurements. Then a break came: he got a job at Bideford Boatyard

Our Wedding day 1969.

at Bank End. His trade was a shipwright and also he was qualified in carpentry. He had also applied to Devonport Dockyard and I would have loved to have gone to Plymouth to live, but unfortunately there were no jobs going at the time. So we started putting roots down in North Devon.

We were still living at Instow, a very nice flat at the Anchorage, fully furnished as we had nothing of our own. Our rent was £5 per week including electric and TV. That was the going rate then as Don's wages as a shipwright was about £20 per week. By the time March came and our six month's lease was up we had found another flat in Westward Ho! which was a permanant one. The day before we left Instow, I cleaned and polished the flat from top to bottom. I wanted to leave it as nice as when we moved in.

I'd just finished when the owner called me downstairs, as someone was at the front door for me. I forgot I'd left the chip pan on the stove, and was longer than I expected. Going back upstairs I was greeted with the whole flat engulfed in black smoke. The tiles on the kitchen ceiling were just melting and dropping. The place was a mess. I was gutted and sat on the stairs and cried my eyes out. The owner sat with me and was very nice about it, saying what had happened had happened; that it was an unfortunate accident, and they would claim on insurance, so I didn't have to touch anything. At least there wasn't a fire but there was a lot of smoke damage and I felt very guilty leaving the next day.

Don's father helped us move. All we owned was able to fit into his car and trailer, we had no furniture, only wedding presents and our clothes. So we moved to our new flat in Westward Ho! in Golden Bay House. Ours was on the very top floor, miles of stairs up, but it was our very own rented place. This time it was empty and we had to furnish it ourselves. We had very little money so we had to do the best we could. We bought a three piece suite from a neighbour of Aunty May in Plympton, for next to nothing and brought it home in the trailer belonging to Don's father. It was our first piece of furniture and very smart. Of course the bedroom furniture was a first priority. I was very glad of 'Grattans' mail order club, where I purchased a lot of our household things on a monthly repayment plan. Gradually we built up our little nest.

Don was now quite established in his job at Bideford Boatyard. He had to cycle to and fro, as we'd had to sell the car being unable to afford it. I started work part-time in a jewelers in Westward Ho! for a while before I had to go into hospital to have a D&C operation. The hospital then was the one near the square in Barnstaple, and was an ancient old building. Needless to say I was so glad to get back to the flat after a few days. Don was a keen darts player and loved to have a night out with the lads, playing in a pub team. Ten shillings was all he took with him for the night out. It paid for his beer, and chips on the way home.

In today's money ten shillings is worth 50 pence. Just after my D&C I fell pregnant with Elysia,seven months after our marriage. It wasn't a very good nine months as I felt sick and had heartburn most of the time. I tried to keep as fit as I could those months, walking a lot around Westward Ho! I refused to take any tablets or medicine of any kind, and didn't touch alcohol. I was never a smoker. Elysia was a breech baby and during the pregnancy the doctors time after time turned her around in the womb, but she kept slipping back to the breech position. At one point I started bleeding and thought I might lose her, so I had to stay in bed for a while.

That Christmas of 1970 we invited Don's mum and dad and his brother Kenneth, for Christmas day lunch. I did all the cooking and it went well apart from the fact I thought something smelt strange, and discovered I'd left the giblets in the plastic bag inside the turkey. It was fine.

Baby wasnt due until February, but late January she decided to come. I started with pains in the early hours of the morning, and by the time Don was ready for work, it was necessary to call the ambulance. Don was unruffled, so it was left to me to go down to the flat below, and ask to use their telephone. The ambulance arrived and packed me off while Don went to work. We couldn't afford him taking time off, plus the fact dad's were not always welcome at the birth in the very early 1970s. Still, I couldn't see him there anyway - he'd have run a mile. I don't remember much about the birth, as I was partly sedated - it was a breech birth - but there were three doctors and what seemed quite a number of midwives. It was lucky that Elysia was only 4½lbs. She arrived on Wednesday 27th January 1971 at mid-day. As soon as she was born they whisked her away to an incubator in the intensive baby care unit. They told me she wasn't breathing properly, and I didn't see her for quite some time. There was no bonding between us and I had no feelings towards her for a while. Poor little dear she looked just like a little prune. Don was so thrilled and phoned everyone. He visited me every evening after work, borrowing his father's car again. I had to stay in for ten days , which was the norm.When I went home I had to leave Elysia behind for a few weeks until she gained some weight. I went to and fro to Barnstaple to see her every day. When we brought her back to the flat, the weather was so cold we had to keep the electric fire on 24/7 for constant heat. We didn't have central heating. She was a baby who loved attention, and drove me to breaking point with her crying. As soon as she was picked up she stopped.

Seeing as we lived on the top floor flat, it was a nightmare dragging the pram up and down. So with the help of my doctor who put in a word for me we were given a council house. Baby was just two months old when we moved to Churchill Road, East-the-Water, Bideford. This time we had to have a removal van, as we couldn't do it ourselves. I felt exhausted moving house and I was still under the weather from giving birth. In fact I went into post natal depression for some time which was not very nice at all. But Don was wonderful. He was caring, and helped me as much as he could with everything. He was always there when I needed him. Back then dad's were not considered for paternity leave, so I coped on my own in those early days until he got home from work. Plus I had no follow up from the hospital, regarding district nurses calling to see if I was coping with baby, or baby's welfare. When we were first married we had a few ups and downs but time now was smoothing the way for better times. Right through life we stood shoulder to shoulder, and weathered every problem together,and grew closer every year. Our love grew more and more as time went on.

We had Elysia christened when she was almost 5 months, in June. Just a small family get together. Aunty May was her godmother and Kenneth her godfather.

We decided to get a dog so they could grow up together, a little pedigree sheltie collie puppy. He was just old enough to leave his mother and it was just like looking after another baby, until we got him house trained. He was such a sweetie, and we called him Brandy. I loved that house - it was lovely and spacious with three bedrooms and such a nice bunch of neighbours all around, who we were friendly with. There was a young couple one side - Dave and Sandra - and Dave was a mate of Dons as they had once worked together on the lorry with the wine company, and also they played darts together. One day he was tragically killed in a car accident, leaving Sandra with two little children.

Sandra decided to move house and his parents moved in at one point. All very close-knit friendly people. Little did we know their eldest son, Michael, would one day marry our little baby daughter Elysia.

Our lifestyle was beginning to improve. Don was working a lot of overtime, and we were able to buy more household things. I bought my first twin tub washing machine as now with the baby there was lots of washing. Up until now I had washed everything by hand, with the help of a baby burco (portable boiler) and a spin dryer.

Wash days were much harder then. It was also none of the disposable nappies, but terry toweling nappies which had to be soaked and washed by hand.

Then in September when Elysia was 8 months old, I was pregnant again with Tracey. This time it was a much more relaxed pregnancy. I felt so much better than the first time There was one false alarm near the end, and I went into hospital but had to come home again. The end of the pregnancy seemed to drag and I wanted it over as it seemed endless.

Barbara my youngest sister was getting married, in Hastings and they were going to make their home there. In my condition I didn't feel like travelling so Don and I didn't go, although I would loved to have. Dad and stepmother Olive didn't go, and by all accounts didn't foot the bill once again. All of us daughters had paid for our own weddings in turn. It was arranged that Don's parents would look after Elysia at their home in Buckland Brewer, while I went into hospital to have Tracey. Don couldn't afford to take time off work, so he was living over there as well. So before it all kicked off, we went over there for my last week or so. While over there I was told the terrible news that Aunty May had suddenly collapsed and died. It was such a shock as I thought a lot of her, and she was Elysia's godmother. It shook and upset me, and I took it badly. That was the Friday, and I think the shock brought on the birth by the following Monday. Sunday night I woke Don to say the baby was coming and once again he had to borrow his dad's car. To our horror there was little petrol in it, and we had to go 16 miles to Barnstaple hospital. We were sweating all the way there in case we ran out of petrol, but thank goodness we made it - no overnight garages then. He got me checked in and couldn't get away fast enough . He hated hospitals, and dad's weren't really welcome until after the birth. So I was in plenty of time, because she wasn't born until much later that Monday on 26th June 1972.

Tracey made her arrival and was put in my arms immediately, not taken away like Elysia was. It was much more relaxed than the first birth, although she was 7½lbs.

Don was the doting dad and came up every evening to see us after he had done a hard day's work. It was a stay of 10 days again before the time came to go home. Don's mother

Olive, and Elysia (who was by then 17 months) came up in the car with Don to pick us up. I felt his mother didn't make any fuss of, or wasn't interested in, the new baby. I found out later they had wanted a grandson. Don's father was always so nice - he felt like more of a father to me than my own dad.

It was happy days bringing up the family. I was as happy as I could possibly be. The happiest I'd ever been. Don was a caring husband and a good dad to the kids. It would be nice if we could bottle those moments and keep them for ever.

One thing about a marriage is to keep it alive and fresh. You have to work at it, and don't let it get stale because that's very often how marriages fail.

When I knew it was the time of day when Don was due home from work, I wanted to look nice for him. Even after the housework and two babies (three if you counted Brandy) to look after, I would stop whatever I was doing to check my appearance, and made sure I looked nice, so he would be glad when he walked through the door.

There's a song that illustrates all this. So even with babies, as then, crawling around and me with my hands in the sink, he would be glad to be home. He would always greet me with a kiss and his pet name for me. He was such a lovely man, so easy to get on with after our first year of settling down and getting used to one another.

There was nothing he wouldn't do for me and the children. He took his share alongside me and really was a wonderful man. I knew I was the luckiest girl in the world.

It was so good, after being alone for so long, to find someone to bond with and make decisions together with. We really became soul mates, and I loved him very much, and I know he loved me, because he told me so many times. For the first time in my life I was really happy, I felt as though I had just started to live.

He was such a romantic at heart. We had Tracey christened, but this time I decided against godparents, as really it means nothing in the long run, and Elysia had already lost one godparent. We had a family party, and it was a lovely day. She was such a happy and contented baby, and I had no trouble with her at all. All the trouble would come later when they got a bit older, then they would both give me the run around.

It must have been the summer of 1976 when we had an exceptionally hot spell of weather, and the reservoirs ran very low, that we were put on standpipes. We had to lug buckets of water from a bowser down the road. I've not known that to happen before nor since. The summers were so much hotter than these later years.

Early in the 70s Don had heard they were taking on workers at Appledore Shipbuilders, he applied for an interview, and was given a job in his trade of shipwright.

It was then things improved moneywise, as he could have as much overtime as he wanted. So he settled in, and he was there for the next 20 years or more.

About this time also, he was getting more involved with darts. He went out one evening to an AGM, saying he wanted to put a few points to the committee, and said he wouldn't be long. After that I knew when he said, 'I won't be long', it was fatal - as he always was. Anyway he came home that evening saying he had been voted onto the committee as competition secretary. It meant a lot of work for him, but he loved it, and he loved his darts. Every season it meant it was his job to order all the trophies for finals night, and we had them in boxes crowding out our spare room for weeks. He did a good job and soon was asked if he'd also like to take on the extra job as league secretary: double the work. He loved it and our phone became a hot line. We got to meet all the top players in the country, as Don invited them down here for special tournaments. Eric Bristow (the crafty cockney), Jocky Wilson, John Lowe, Keith Dellar, the list goes on.

After a while, he took over running the *News of the World* darts, for the North Devon section, taking a player to Exeter for the quarter finals. I always used to go with him. We were both invited to London for the finals which was in Wembley arena and later on was staged at Canary Wharf. These events were always televised, and one year our girls said they saw Don and myself in the audience. After the finals were over, we joined a large group of people in the Wembley Conference Centre for a very lavish meal: management, players, and wives. Don got to meet all the players and was in his element, chatting to them all. All our expenses for the weekend were taken care of by the *News of the World* : train fare, top hotel, food and drinks. We did these weekends for quite a number of years until the paper decided to finish the event.

We bought a car from Wendy (Don's sister) and Brian (her husband) to get around, our first for a long time, although Don had a motor bike to travel to work. We had been without one for a long time, and it made life so much easier for me, as our house was all uphill from town, pushing two babies in the pram.

Until they were of school age Elysia and Tracey gave me the run around, and kept me on my toes, getting into endless amounts of mischief - too much to write about. Elysia was always the ring leader, and Tracey just followed. I remember one incident where they were playing in the back garden with their trikes, I was inside, and everything suddenly went quiet. Looking out the front bedroom window, I saw them disappearing over the brow of Pollyfields, riding their trikes as fast as they could pedal, the dog behind them, heading in the direction of town. I had to drop everything and race after them. Another time after I had tied the garden gate to keep her in Elysia climbed over, falling and cutting her eyebrow, and I had to take her to surgery to get it stitched. Another time I caught her putting sand in the air vents of the car.

Oh Lordy Lordy!

Tracey loved school, but Elysia hated it, I'd often find her sitting on the back door step at lunch-time, when I came home from my morning job.

When they were little, for extra cash, I worked three evenings a week at a small hotel in Northam, in the kitchen. It was a nice break getting some adult company as well. I only intended to go for a season's work, but eventually stayed for eight years, changing to mornings when they started full time school at 5 years. The only trouble was the holiday time, I had no-one to leave them with so I had to take them with me, and they hated it. One or two of the staff weren't very nice about it, but I would never quit because of such people. I would never let anyone get the better of me. As I have said before if anyone leaves it's not going to be me.

While the children were still very young I developed health problems. Because of a suspected blood clot in my shoulder I had to take warfarin for quite some time and it didn't improve, so I was sent to Bristol hospital for tests. I had to have a scan on my veins, which consisted of a wire inserted into a vein in my groin and fed up to my heart and a dye injected and monitored on a screen. No clot was found. I was in Bristol for a few days and was glad to get home again.

Don on the other hand never seemed to have anything more than colds bother him, apart from once when he was in terrible pain in his ribs. It turned out he had an abscess between his ribs, but at the time , it was thought he had broken a rib he was off work quite some time until it healed. Time off work was something he didn't like he was never still at home, always doing DIY couldn't sit still for long, could always see when something needed doing.

We rarely went on holidays apart from going down to Cornwall to visit Aunt Leda or Gloria. When it was summer school holidays and Don was on holiday from the dock, I always tried to organize day trips away. Trips to the theatre shows in Plymouth and Paignton.I did organize a couple of trips over to the Isles of Scilly.

One of those trips we stayed overnight at Gloria's in St Ives and catching the 6.30 Scillonian from Penzance. This was a nostalgic trip for Don as he was a shipwright that had worked on the Scillonian when it was built at Appledore. The weather that day was hot and sunny and the girls were disappointed they didn't have their swimsuits

Tracey was sea sick going over, but recovered when we got there to enjoy the day. She was fine on the way back, if I remember she was prone to car travel sickness as well.We took in the Island coach tour and made most of the day, saying it would be nice to come back for a longer stay. The day really wasn't long enough, as we had to return when the Scillonian left later in the afternoon.It was so peaceful and tranquil over there,and the sea was so clear and blue.

We used to go down to Fraddon as often as we could manage and invite Aunt Leda up to stay with us, especially at Christmas. I didn't like to think of her being on her own.

One day Don brought home a kitten from work, the mother cat the work crew had adopted and fed, had had three kittens and the lads were trying to find homes for them.

We thought it would be nice for Tracey to have a pet, seeing as Elysia had a dog. So it became Brandy the dog and Whiskey the cat. We had Whiskey for quite a number of years, before she became ill with a terminal growth and had to be put to sleep. Tracey was devastated, naturally enough. The vet pointed out maybe it wasn't the right moment, but two little kittens (brothers) had been handed in to be rehomed, and we asked Tracey to think it over and decide if she would like one. It didn't take her long and Elysia said she would like the other. I thought it would be nice if they were given a home together. So we ended up with our family extended.

The girls named them Bobby and Lucky, both black cats, lovely natures, and very gentle. Brandy had to get used to the new additions, which he did, and he was so good with them. They literally walked all over him especially when they all curled up in front of the fire.

While we were at Churchill Road I developed more health problems. It was quite worrying at the time and over a long period of time. It was decided I should have an operation and have a wedge of tissue from one of my breasts. When the results came back it was cancer negative, so sighs of relief. Although it relieved a lot of pain the situation was still there and I discovered through reading a magazine about Oil of

Aunt Leda, with Elysia and Tracey, also Brandy in 1972.

Evening Primrose and that really was the answer. Life was made so much better and the pain is now minimised.

Again while we were still at Churchill Road Don's father was rushed into hospital with a heart attack which turned out to be fatal. He was such a nice man, and more of a father to me than my own father. Don took it all in his stride: not a man of outward emotions, he kept a lot of his feelings to himself.

Then, in the early in the nineteen eighties - 1982 to be exact, when Maggie Thatcher decided everyone could buy their council house, we considered it. We had it valued but thought at the time that if we wanted to ever sell on again, it may be difficult as it was a council house. Also we were beginning to have bother with the neighbours both sides. On one side, the family we had got along with had moved, and another family had moved in. On the other side, the family we had been friends with for a long time, their children had grown up into teenagers, and showed no consideration about noise levels, with their music.

It had become such a headache living between the two that we decided to move on and buy privately. So we bought a two bedroom house in Woolsery, 9 miles from Bideford. It had only been built about 2 years previously. It was a lovely house in Manor Park, but proved to have a lot of teething problems with one thing and another. We spent a lot of money on it, and Don did a lot of work on and around it. We had a Parkray central heating system fitted and Don installed secondary double glazing. With the help of his brother he built a porch at the back, cemented out the back garden, and erected a shed. Don spent many hours re-styling the front gardens and, because this time we had a garage, Don started making his home brew beer, bottling it up and storing it. Boy, it was it strong stuff! One very cold winter some of the bottles exploded and it was a good job they missed spraying the car as the smell of beer hangs on.

The thing with pets and moving home is that they get confused with their surroundings. So when we first arrived there,the girls took the cats outside on leads for a few days to familiarise them. One evening we let Brandy out in the back garden to do his business, up to then Don hadn't fixed a gate. When we went to call him in, he had disappeared. It was late and dark, and we spent ages out, searching and calling, but couldn't find him.I put his bed out by the back door, when we went to bed in case he wandered back. All this upset me, and I kept going down to see if he'd returned, but no. Next morning I went around the lanes calling, and looking, but no joy. When the postman arrived he said he'd seen him up the lane, and he knew he was ours and tried to catch him but couldn't. So I again went up the lane looking for him, worried in case he got in a field with sheep, as a farmer can quite legally shoot a dog if it's worrying the flock. But no he couldn't be found. When the girls came home from school, they were upset he wasn't back. As soon as Don came home he went looking again, this time with luck.He saw him way up the lane, and whistled. Brandy knew that whistle and came running. He was so dirty and tired, poor love, and was glad to be home; as glad as we were. I remember his eyes were so heavy with tiredness. He enjoyed all the fuss we made of him. Needless to say we took measures to make sure it didn't happen again.

The cats used to spend hours, down in the trees at the back of the houses. They were hunters, often bringing home little presents,very often half-eaten slow-worms. I used to cringe as I disposed of them.

While we were living at Woolsery, Don had three motor cycle accidents, two being caused through pot holes in the back lanes, the other caused by a stupid woman driving her car out from a side lane into the side of the motorcycle, causing him to skid and slam into a brick wall. Poor Don he was terribly shook up, bruised and battered. Needless to say he started getting nervous about riding the bike again. I felt very angry towards that stupid woman who was a bad driver at the best of times, and a very nervous driver too. We had a car, but I needed it most days to get to work, or to get to town for appointments. Don only took it when I didn't need it.

I still had my job in Bideford mornings at Yeolden House Hotel, and also I got myself another part time job at Hoops Inn at Horns Cross. So it was mornings in Bideford, come home do the housework and evening meal, then out again in the evenings to Hoops. Sometimes doing the weekly shop between jobs. This was all due to the cost of the mortage, and we found we were on a tight budget for the first few years. There were rumours that Appledore Shipbuilders might be laying men off because it was difficult getting orders. The worry of this plus Don's accident, didn't help him, and he went through a bad patch of nerves and depression, and was on medication and home off work for a while.

He came through it, the rumours were unfounded, the orders flowed, and the work kept going. Later at one

Summer 1982. Don and myself on a visit to Minehead

point a gang of workers including Don were sent from Appledore Shipbuilders to Falmouth docks for a week. It was quite good financially as it was double time, and accommodation paid for, but I missed him.

We had a holiday at Pontins, Brean Sands, Burnham-on-Sea which was a nice break for a week. We enjoyed all four of us together, and there was plenty to do there daytimes and evenings. I remember the girls decided they'd like to each take out a pedal boat on the lake deciding halfway around that one should try and step over into the other one's boat - with almost disastrous results. I can't remember which one of them fell overboard in the water, but luckily it wasnt very deep. Soon we saw the funny side of it as we went back to our chalet for a change of clothing.

While we were away a neighbour was feeding the cats and shutting them up in our shed at night. The only thing was that Bobby had decided it was his turn to disappear and by the time we got back he was gone. We thought we'd lost him when after days of painstaking search, he turned up dragging himself home. He'd caught a virus and was very ill and must have must have lain in one of the hedges we'd previously searched. We were overjoyed to see him and gave him lots of TLC. Tracey had him on her bed for a week nursing him better.

I enjoyed the village life at Woolsery, as did Don and the girls, out in the country with plenty of nice walks. The neighbours were all very nice and friendly, which is the best part of small communities. But it was becoming apparent after a few years, that we needed to make a change. So after living there for 5 years we decided, in 1987, that we should make the move back into Bideford. It was increasingly awkward for Don travelling to and from work, and getting so cold on his motor bike. He used to arrive home as white as a sheet, and shivering from head to toe. Winters were absolutely freezing cold, with plenty of snow and ice. I kept a spare pantry for emergency in case we were snowed in, with oil lamps as the electricity seemed to go down quite often. Plus the girls were at an age when they needed their own bedroom, as often war was declared due to their sharing. Elysia very often decided she'd had enough and would take off on her bicycle wanting to leave home. She'd get lost and I'd have to go and look for her and bring her home with her bike in the car. We decided, beside these points, that it would be a long way for them to travel to jobs when they left school. By now Elysia was playing truant from school, apparently quite regularly, of which I was unaware, until one day the school rang me. Often she would pretend to catch the school bus, but actually spend the days down in the wooded area at the back of the houses, where the cats used to join her, she confessed to me later. I often wondered where the cats were all day. Then when the school bus was due home she'd emerge from the woods and arrive back up the lane with them all, including Tracey, who never let on what she was up to.

Before we made the house move back into Bideford, we'd lost our dear Brandy, who was then about 14 years of age. He was looking old, his legs weren't so good, started getting arthritis and had become incontinent. Sometimes if we all went for a walk Don very often carried him home. One morning I came down to find Brandy having a heart attack - Elysia and I carried him to the car on a blanket into the vets in Bideford. The vet said he really was very ill, and I had to make the awful decision to let them put him to sleep. We were losing one of the family, and we were all devastated. It took a very long time for the hurt to heal. I kept a little tuft of his fur in a small box with my jewellery for years. He was a wonderful companion and we all loved him.

So in 1987 we bought and moved into a house in Bideford, only intending it to be a stepping stone back into Bideford, and to carry on looking for a property preferably with a garage. It became a time when the market started slowing, and not many properties were selling. We had put ours on the market but couldn't sell, so after a while we gave up and decided to stay. It was nice being back in town and Don sold his motor cycle buying a Robin Reliant car, which gave him a bit more comfort - plus it was cheap to run. His workmates used to tease him, calling it the 'Plastic Pig!'

The girls were glad to be in town also and Tracey did a YTS (Youth Training Service) job in a gift shop when she first left school. She then took a factory job as a machinist in Barnstaple for a company who made underwear for Marks and Spencer. She bought herself a Lambretta Scooter to travel back and forth. She passed her test quickly and enjoyed her travelling until one day, during the bad winter, a neighbour had decided to wash his car in the street. The temperature was below freezing with the result that the road became a sheet of ice. Tracey came home and skidded, frightening herself so badly that she wouldn't ride her scooter again.

So at that point she decided the next step was to buy a car which was more practical, passing her test first time after just a few months.

Elysia had one or two jobs when she first left school, then decided to apply for a job at the same factory as Tracey and her application was successful. From then on they travelled every day together. After they were there for some time Marks and Spencer decided to take their factory work overseas, but both girls left before the factory actually closed.

We'd only been living in Bideford for about a year when I'd had a phone call to say my cousin Graham in Plymouth had died suddenly of a heart attack. It was a terrible shock as he was only 40 years old and a lovely man. About six months later Aunt Leda died. We used to go down to see her as much as possible and had brought her up to North Devon to spend time with us especially at Christmas. The cancer had come back over time, and in the end it raged right through her. She spent her last few days in a hospice in St Austell, where she was looked after with great care. We had gone down to see her on the Sunday, and on the Monday we had a call to say she'd passed away. It broke my heart and I took a long time to get over it. She was one person in my life who was always there for me, and helped me in every way she could. I knew there was always a home there if ever I needed one. It's always sad at times like this but unfortunately 'where there's a will there's a relative' and often people begin to circle, wondering if they now have an interest in the property of the deceased.

The first thing Uncle Eddie did was to visit Aunt Leda's solicitor to find out what she'd left him even before the funeral, or the reading of the will afterwards. He was told she had left him £200 only. This was an amount he had given grandpa once to help out. When he knew this he was not happy and washed his hands of everything; cancelled the flowers he had ordered, and refused to attend the funeral. He came to Aunt Leda's house later, while we were with the solicitor having the will read to us. He only came to pick up a portable TV he had once lent her. He was an awful brother to her in life so in death she repaid him. He could never have enough material-wise, Uncle Eddie, it was all take and money grabbing, but 'you can't take it with you'.

Gloria and myself were the only family that used to care about Aunt Leda otherwise she would have been totally alone, apart from some good neighbours.

Barbara and John for example used to come down from Hastings to Cornwall to visit dad, passed her door but never called to see her. After Aunt Leda died both John and Barbara turned up looking around the house to see if there was anything they could pick up. I was so disgusted I had to walk out of the house to cool off. Eventually the house was sold privately, and the contents taken to an auction. I thought at the time it was very sad: it took a lifetime to collect, and everything sold off in minutes.

Gloria and myself were executors of the will, and we worked closely with the solicitor. Everything was divided equally between Barbara, Gloria, and myself. I said all along Barbara didn't deserve her share.

It seemed awful afterwards to see someone else living in the two houses - our home from birth, and which had been in the family for so long.

Writing all this it seems we had lots of problems, but that's part of life. Don and I had a good social life, went out always together to the usual round of darts events all over the county. There were theatre trips, cinema, and out for meals.

Life on the whole was good, as we made it good. Don's mother - now a widow living on her own in sheltered accommodation - was a worry to her daughter Queenie. An unfounded worry really as she was quite happy and independent. But Queenie decided her mother should go into a home, and being the bossy boots of the family she went ahead and made all the arrangements. And though not all the family were in agreement, on settling her into a home, Queenie then announced that we all had to pay a share for her monthly bill of a few hundred pounds. Don and I disagreed right from the start as did other members of the family and this put a split right down the family, though some

I'm sure went along with Queenie for a quiet life. So this was the parting of the way for us and Queenie. As it happened I was working in the very same residential home. It didn't suit Don's mother - not really - in the fact she lost not only her independence, but had no exercise, was just sitting around doing nothing but eat, which in turn made her gain weight.

Within a few years she died. I'd started working at the home when we'd moved into Bideford from Woolsery in 1987. I enjoyed working there and made some good friends.

In 1989 Don and I decided that now we'd been left a little money in Aunt Leda's will that we would take a holiday. This was somewhat alien to us, as we never had much money to spend especially on holidays. We took a Cosmos Coaches package tour over to Europe - six countries in eight days. It was quite a whistle-stop journey, living out of suitcases and moving on: Belgium, Austria, Switzerland, Germany, Italy and France. We weren't too keen on the German food.

I remember we took a lovely boat trip out on Lake Lucern; took in a show in Paris - it went all too quick. We now had a taste for travel and enjoyed it. The following year in 1990 just by chance we read in the local paper of a certain trip to Florida. It looked too good to miss and Don urged me to ring up and book for all of us this time. We covered the cost of the holiday and the girls could save for their own spending money, as they were both working. It was part coach tour starting at Bideford to Heathrow airport, before flying to Orlando and meeting up with our rep and fellow passengers there. This tour was for seventeen days. It was late October early November, but it was really hot. Our hotel was on International drive, just a short way from all the attractions, including Disney. On the first day we celebrated Halloween at Church Street Station in Orlando, a well known hot spot for shops, bars, etc., and it was a fantastic evening.

Halloween is really celebrated in the USA. Don and I went on our own, leaving the girls to have time on their own. They really don't know what they missed! The next two days we spent in Disney World and the Epcot centre and these places

November 1990. Don and myself in Miami en route to Florida Keys

are fabulous for both young and old. We had a fantastic time and during our few days in Orlando we took excursions, including Bush Gardens (a theme-type safari park). Then another day to Sea World. Another day, another excursion to the Kennedy Space Centre, at Cape Canaveral which I can only describe as surreal. We were taken all over the centre to see the rocket sites and, surprising enough, a lot of wild life abounds. I remember we visited the Imax theatre, the screen being about two stories high, and watching a space documentary about everything from rocket take-off and being above the Earth watching the astronauts doing their work outside of the space-ships. The screen was so huge it felt as though we were in space as we watched it. That day was fantastic. Then it was off to Fort Lauderdale for a couple of days, then on to Key West, Florida. We stopped for a drink in Sloppy Joe's, a famous pub. I loved all the quaint shops: outside one was a placard saying 'SHOPLIFTERS WILL BE CONGRATULATED AND THEN SHOT.'

We saw the house that the writer Ernest Hemingway once owned.

Florida is very much the home of the alligator and we took a hover-boat ride out onto the waterway marshes to see the wildlife. At one point when the engines were cut the alligators came right up to the boat. These creatures have been pushed further away as more land is drained, and people move in. We had some time in Miami walking on the long white sandy beaches. A lot of Miami buildings seemed to be 1930s dated and painted all the delicate shades of the rainbow!

Soon we headed up the coast to St Petersburg where we had a few days relaxing. Our hotel was right on the beach.

Then it was on again heading eventually to New Orleans, and en route we stopped in the capital Tallahassee, just a brief stop, where I got the impression it was a very legal, commerce-type city, and very busy. We went on to stay in Mobile overnight before our final leg. After we left there and half way to New Orleans Tracey discovered she had left her camera in the hotel bedroom. Later we phoned them, but it hadn't been handed in so she bought another one and made an insurance claim on her lost one.

Then it was our last stop: New Orleans! Such a vibrant place, alive with music. Music everywhere you turned, in every street. The old Mississippi music, Creole-style, and the old Blues of the negro. The whole place buzzed. We had a choice to make: a Mississippi River Boat trip or to explore the town, and we did the latter. We stopped for some lunch, and a sit down as Elysia had developed a bad headache. I decided to try the local dish of Jumbalia, but didn't like it much and was a bit disappointed. Still, we did loads of shopping: so much so that Elysia had to buy another suitcase. Our excursion one day took us around the city and one stop was at a cemetery. It was explained that no-one was buried underground, as, if it flooded the coffins would just float up. So they were sealed above ground.

One evening with a group of our travelling friends we were taken to Bourbon Street, to a Creole-style Jazz Club, then on to another Cabaret night spot. We had been told it would be in our best interest if we didn't leave our hotel at night on our own, as there were many unsavoury characters wandering the streets.

Our hotel, The Carlton, was one of the best in the heart of the city, and quite luxurious. It was hard having to pack to come home, as our holiday was coming to an end.

We had to fly from New Orleans to New York to catch a connecting flight back to Heathrow. On leaving New Orleans just into the flight the captain announced a fault and that we'd have to go back and in doing so, we'd have to dump fuel. Then came the next announcement - a change of plan - we'd need to fly on to Atlanta for repairs. Then the third announcement! The fault was rectified and we could proceed to New York. These were the days when I had become nervous of flying, which I suppose comes with age,there's no fear when you're young. The girls knew how I felt and teased me, saying, 'Look mum! Bruce Willis is out there on the wing!'

Although it was a good night-flight home, I was glad to get my feet on the ground.

After we came back from Florida, we decided changes needed making to the house. We had a little money left from Aunt Leda's will so decided to put it to good use. Soon it was all systems go. We had a Parkray and Central Heating installed, and new carpets fitted throughout the house. A new kitchen, and double glazing plus a new style bathroom. Don re-styled the back garden making a paved patio. This was real hard work on Don so Brian very kindly helped him.

It was after we had the double glazing installed, that AGS asked us if we'd like to make a TV commercial for them. We agreed we'd do it -the only thing was that Don couldn't be there on the day they wanted to shoot, so I said I'd carry on and do it on my own. The film crew turned up in three transit vans and the house was filled with their people. I had to be made-up by their crew. It took about an hour to shoot, yet when the advert went out on TV it lasted about three minutes.

Everybody kept saying 'I saw you on TV!'

Time went on, and all of us were developing headaches,and feeling sick,this went on for some time,until one night I woke to go to the bathroom and collapsed on the floor, feeling sick and faint. Lucky we always slept with the window open, I threw it open wider, stuck my head out, and recovered.

We contacted our plumber who had put the heating system in, who told us carbon monoxide was creeping through the bricks of the chimney into our bedroom. He hadn't put a liner in the chimney when he did the job. So we had the expense then of having to put in a ceramic liner the whole length of the chimney. We could have, all of us, died at any time before this was done.

It wasn't long into 1991 after we returned from Florida that Elysia and I had a disagreement, and she moved out - getting a horrible flat in town; nothing much more than a squat.

Relations were strained and shortly after Tracey, too, decided she wanted to move out and join Elysia. She had been only gone a few hours when she came back realising it wasn't so great a move. She now delighted in the fact she could have Elysia's room,which was much bigger than hers.

Some time later on Tracey again thought she'd like her own place, but this time asked me to come and help her choose a flat. She decided on one in town, and I helped her move in with all her stuff.

Don and I thought that was it: we'd now have the place to ourselves. However, just one week later she came home and asked if she could move back. She said she had made a mistake, and didn't like living on her own. So of course we said she could, and once more I helped her move all her stuff back. Needless to say she lost her deposit.

Elysia was different: she had made the break and was glad, decorating her flat and buying a few things to make it better.

Don had been over there working and was walking back home when he suddenly felt ill.

Luckily Tracey was home, and drove him up to Bideford Hospital and contacted me as I was at work in Instow. I arrived at the local hospital just as he was being whisked by ambulance to Barnstaple, so I followed by car. At first they thought he'd suffered a heart attack as the pain was in his chest. He was kept in and given lots of tests,and kept under observation. The results of these tests pointed to the fact he had an enlarged prostate gland, and it had effected all the glands in his body. The doctors couldn't operate until everything had settled, so he had to come home and have a period of rest.

After a few months of rest he went back in for his operation and during his recovery I used to go in every day and sit with him until the end of visiting from 3-30pm until 8-30pm. I used to go down to the staff canteen for my tea,while he was having his. I couldn't bear to be apart from him even for one day. We were told by the doctor the operation was a success and there was nothing to worry about so we were very relieved. After a while he went back to work, but used to come home very tired,and said his legs felt as though they were dropping off, and had backache.

Our GP told him he was entitled to take early retirement if he wanted and would sign all the necessary papers, but Don couldn't understand why the GP had said he could retire early. He felt he wasn't ready to give up work, and so life carried on as usual for a while; working and playing darts.

In 1993 one day I had an appointment at the surgery, and before leaving, just happened to ask the GP, 'How long will Don have to keep taking his tablets? The ones prescribed for him on leaving the hospital?'

The doctor looked at me very strangely and said, 'But they are to control the Cancer.' I felt sick. Stunned and shocked, as we had no idea, no-one had told us. I had to go and face him in the waiting room, as we had planned to go shopping. The doctor was stunned that we hadn't been told at the

1993. Don's last darts final - he's on stage shaking hands.

hospital. Don had no idea, and I had to face him with that knowledge. I couldn't tell him; my heart was breaking, but I had to 'put on a face'. I felt I couldn't tell anyone this secret and wondered what to do. I cried behind his back, then had to appear bright in front of him. After holding the secret for about three months from Don I approached the doctor again and said 'I cant bear it any longer'.

He said, 'Don *has* to be told" and that he would do it. At the appointment Don next had, I went with him. I was dreading it, and sat in the waiting room. When he came out, and as we got in the car he said, 'You *know* don't you?' We came home, and I thought he was going to have a breakdown. It was the end of the world for us, and it was horrible. He thought about it and said he would tell the girls as they had a right to know, but otherwise he didn't want anyone else to know. The poor girls didn't know what had hit them; the bottom fell out of their world, as they loved their dad. Keeping the secret from everyone especially the rest of the family was very hard.

Everything was going wrong, as another blow was about to hit. The cats were both due for their annual booster injections,and we were told their teeth needed cleaning. We left them at the vets one morning for their general anaesthetic, and to have their teeth done. About an hour later came a phone call to say Lucky had died under the anaesthetic. Lucky was Elysia's cat and Tracey immediately said the vet was not to go ahead with Bobby. The night before I'd had a bad premonition about this but thought I was being silly. This was another heartbreak - Don loved the cats as we all did and he took it badly.

After a while Don decided it wasn't a good idea keeping the fact he had cancer a secret any longer. He'd just not wanted sympathy from anyone. So now he made the decision he was going to give up darts after nineteen years on the committee. He'd made an enormous amount of friends, and was very well liked and respected. That Christmas was very unhappy for us, we went through the motions, but sadness was eating us up inside. Considering the situation Don put on a brave face in public, went out and faced the world, and laughed, but I knew only too well how he was feeling inside. He really was so courageous. When Christmas 1993 and New Year were out of the way Don said, 'Let's have a break away from it all.' So we consulted the travel brochures and decided on Malta for two weeks. A little bit of sun.

The day we left for the airport in February 1994, it was so cold and had snowed. We hired a car to take us to Exeter airport, had a good flight over, and checked into our hotel - The Preluma, which was right on the seafront at Sliema. The trip was just what we needed: we tried to forget everything and enjoy some sightseeing around the island. We met up with another couple who were from Tiverton on the arrival bus in Malta. Les and Margaret are a lovely couple, we used to meet up with them on excursions and in the hotel in the evenings for a drink. One excursion will remain with me for as long as I live, this being our day trip to Gozo the sister island of

Malta. We took the ferry over and had a lovely day, visiting Medina - the silent city - where there are no cars. It's situated very high up and you can see for miles, probably it was a good vantage point years ago, to see advancing enemies. There were so many invasions from the Moors and Turks etc. During the second world war the island didn't escape. It played host to a lot of our troops and was a haven for our ships. Afterwards Malta was awarded the George Cross.

One little church on Gozo which people go to they call *The Miracle Church* because of the frequency of miracles there over the years. During the war a bomb hit the church and finished up in the middle of it, but it failed to explode, was defused and is still there today for everyone to see. The day we visited had started out as a really nice day and the weather was lovely. It was when we were on the ferry back to the mainland that the weather changed. It was fine when we left, with no indication of what was to come. The sky turned black and the wind got up. We were in for a rough ride back. The nearer we got to the shores of Malta, the worse the storm got. We were tossed like a cork. Storms get up very quickly in the Med,very changeable. I honestly thought my time had come and was terrified as was everyone else. I openly prayed to God to look after us. We held on tight to a pillar in the passenger lounge to stop sliding from one end of the boat to the other. Others who couldn't get a hold were sliding and falling all over the place as was all the furniture; tables and chairs flying. As we were being tossed around all we could see was the sky out of one side of the boat and sea out of the other, before being thrown the other way. We were told the captain may have to abort our original docking port and try for another one on the leeward side of the coast, but then decided he'd attempt the original one. Even then when we got to the dockside we couldn't tie up as the waves kept the boat rising and falling and no way would the cars be able to get off the ramp. So those without cars - foot passengers tried to filter off the boat, by jumping when the waves lowered and came level with the slipway. That's when Don and myself, Margaret and Les got off. I vowed I'd never set foot on a boat again. It was so good to get back on dry land.

During the holiday the Maltese people were so nice, and the weather was so much warmer than back home. We visited quite a lot of places on the island, so many churches and places of worship. The break did us good and on the whole there were good days and bad days. When back at the hotel Don would break down and cry in the privacy of our room, and we'd sit together and I'd hold him and give him all the support I could. I had to keep my feelings under control and be strong for him. I loved him so much and it broke my heart to see him like that. He said he wouldn't tell Margaret and Les about his cancer and spoil their holiday, but would do so if we kept in touch when we got back home. Most holiday friendships are forgotten once the holiday was over, but this one was to be different. We did keep in touch and they both proved to be wonderful friends. When we got back home and all met up again Don told them of his illness: they were shocked as they'd had no idea.

We had only been back 24 hours when I had a phone-call from Gloria to say my dad had died, and had been buried. I had no idea he had even been ill. Again it was prostate cancer. Gloria had known we were so torn apart with Don's illness so it was kept from me, especially as dad and I never did see eye to eye, and there was no love lost between us. So it meant there hadn't even been any flowers from me. I don't think dad ever cared about his daughters, nor his grandchildren.

I tried to keep Don's mind busy and we travelled around a bit. By now I'd given up my job to be with him 24/7. It really didn't seem fair. We had a good marriage and had been content: of course there had been ups and downs, but life had been good and he always made me happy.

We decided our car had seen better days, and realised we could go for the option of a mobility car, so we got a little Renault Clio. All we had to worry about was putting the petrol in; everything else was taken care of. It made life so much easier for us.

This year, 1994, was our 25th Silver Wedding anniversary on 6th September. So we thought it would be nice if we did something special. We decided to have a dinner party at the Royal Hotel in Bideford and invited some family members as well as Les and Margaret. This was on the Saturday, but on the Thursday before, in the evening, Elysia and Tracey told us to get dressed up as a taxi was coming to take us all out. We had no idea where we were going. The taxi stopped outside the Liberal Club in Bideford's High Street and we were taken in. Inside we were astounded to see all our family and friends at a surprise party which the girls had organized. They had gone to a lot of trouble contacting everyone and had sent invites out, booked a buffet, and a disco. It was really such a wonderful surprise, and we had so many lovely gifts that we had to go out and buy a cabinet to house them all!

The previous week I'd suffered a slipped disc again in my back, and I struggled all week. The time I should have been enjoying myself I had a job to move around. By the time everyone was leaving for home on the Sunday Don and myself were confined to bed, him with his problems and me with mine. I've still kept all the lovely cards we were given - such lovely memories.

Life would never be the same again for us. Some days were better than others for Don, but his pain became increasingly worse and his medication had to be increased. Early in the year of 1995, in May, we decided to rent a cottage in Cornwall for a week, and I remember it was still very cold weather, and we had to wrap up.

Having wrapped up, we got around to a few places of interest, and spent one day over with Gloria and Nicky, who were very supportive to us.

It wasn't really a very good break, Don cried most of the time and I did my best to support him, but we both knew things were getting worse.

Friends and family were also really supportive at this time of our life. The family doctor gave Don the best attention and support he could possibly give, and took good care of him. Don started going to the Hospice in Barnstaple as a day patient one morning a week. There was no bedded unit there at that time. He was very unsure to start with, as he thought it would be all doom and gloom. But it was the other way around. Everyone was made to feel very welcome and a lot of laughter went on; the staff were wonderful and cheerful. The facility was a large rambling house which had been left to the Hospice Trust by some well to do, very generous people and acres of ground went with it; beautiful gardens and wildlife. Don loved to take his video camera with him and walk the grounds on the days he went there. He had a hospice support nurse, Rosemary, who came to visit him at home and she was such an angel, giving him incredible support and besides helping to manage his medicine, also helped him with any paperwork that needed to be done.

I don't think we would have coped if it was not for her help.

Margaret and Les were a great source of support to us even though they lived as far away as Tiverton. They used to visit and phone us often, and proved to be real friends.

Don and I tried to make life as good as it could be while we still had time, but time was running out. Soon his pain was again worsening and the drugs had to be continually increased. His doctor suggested he should be admitted to hospital in Bideford for a while to regulate his drugs while at the same time giving me some respite, and although we tried this it didn't work. He didn't like being on the ward with other sick people and became depressed and would cry. We didn't like being separated from each other, so I would spend all day every day with him. This drove me to exhaustion. We were both glad when he came home.

He had to travel to Exeter hospital some days to have chemotherapy which would make him so ill that for days after the treatment he was sick. It came to the point where we decided it would be better if he had a bed downstairs. So that was it, and he started on the downward scale. I found it increasingly difficult as each time he needed turning in bed, I couldn't manage with my back. We got to the point when he tearfully decided he should go into hospital. So late in August 1995 he was admitted to Bideford hospital. The nurses and our doctor gave him the best possible care and were absolutely wonderful. September 6th came, our 26th wedding anniversary, and the staff put on a lovely tea for us. Don's bed-space was filled with flowers. I stayed with him from first thing in the morning until last thing at night, each day from then on. Everything else had to take second place. The hospital were so good as to give me a room and a bed where I could sleep, so that I could be close to him.

Elysia and Michael were living in Plymouth at this point and as Don was getting so ill they came and stayed at our house. Elysia told him she was pregnant and he said he was glad to hear the news, and was happy for them.

In the last week of his life Don said he would like to make amends with his sister Queenie, so Wendy and I went over to see her and asked if she'd like to see her brother, probably for the last time, and before it was too late. She said she had a headache and turned the idea down saying, 'I couldn't care less whether or not he's six feet under right now.' I replied by saying, 'I hope your soul rots in hell.' It was heartbreaking to tell Don that she didn't want to see him. With tears in his eyes he said 'It's her loss.'

I suppose I neglected everyone and everything at this point in time, except Don. I knew I was losing him and I knew he was fighting to live. I loved him so much it was tearing me apart. I cried so much but had to put on a brave face for him. Our love was deep and we were being torn apart; over the years we had become one - soul mates. Only someone who has gone through it could realise how I felt.

I asked the Minister to come and sit with him. He took both our hands and blessed us. I think Don seemed calmer afterwards.

The evening before he died, he kept saying about the light, and looked up and said 'He's up there waiting for me.'

Don had fought so long and was now exhausted, and was about to give in. On the night of Friday 13th September 1995 at midnight, or a little after into the 14th, Don gave up his fight and passed away. I had been sleeping in the bed next to him in the ward for the last few days, so I was with him at the end. I stayed with him as long as I could stroking his hair, with him still warm beside me.

Then I knew it was all over, and it would be the last time I saw him, and I had to leave him forever. I walked out of the ward in a cold daze. I felt numb and emotionless I couldn't feel anything. I couldn't cry, just had a sense of release, for him and his pain. The family came up at that point. It was paticularly hard on Elysia and Tracey, they had thought the world of their dad and now he was gone. Tracey went into the ward with a nurse to see him, and I remember she screamed out, 'That's not my dad!' and broke down. Elysia was different, she wanted to remember him from better days. In fact she hadn't seen him at all in the previous week, so determined was she to remember him as he used to be, although he longed to have seen her, looking up each time the door opened in case it was her.

After the funeral we all went back to the Liberal Club for the wake: all his many friends and colleagues were at both. I was approached by a member of the club asking could they have permission to set up an Annual Memorial Cup for darts in Don's name. Of course, I agreed as it was something I had intended to do, but they had beaten me to it. So that was the start of playing for his cup every year, and I decided he would like it if the proceeds were to go to the Hospice. Many thousands have now been raised, thanks to a dedicated darts committee. I went to these events over many years,and he was regarded as 'the best'.

After the funeral when things had settled down, I laid his ashes to rest as he wanted in the peaceful beautiful grounds of the Hospice, with the permission of the Trust.

5

Now I had to face life alone again, after so many years of planning everything together. I felt so alone. I had to start making decisions on my own, I couldn't, I just fell apart and felt I was walking in a dream. I felt numb and zombie-like, for a very long time. All the love had gone, and he wasn't there to put his arms around me, to comfort and reassure me. Whenever I felt down, he had always been there for me, but now no more. All through this period of time Don's sister Wendy was there for me, and she was my rock. Elysia and Michael went back to Plymouth again, leaving myself and Tracey here.

Friction grew between Tracey and myself. She said that I had changed, and for the worse. There were frequent arguments and falling-outs. There were times she wouldn't speak to me for weeks on end. Instead of bonding together during our bereavement, we did the opposite. Seven months on and into May, Elysia gave birth to Jade Coral. It was the first bit of joy we'd had in a long time.

It was wonderful being a grandparent, and I loved her to bits. Elysia and Michael wanted to come back to Bideford to live where all their family and friends were. So as a stepping stone I offered to breech the gap and let them stay with me until they got a property. It wasn't an ideal situation, all piled in together, and things didn't always run smoothly, but I was willing to put up with it for their benefit, and thought it would work out in the end. Quite soon they found a property to rent in Woolsery, on the same estate where Elysia had lived as a child. Jade was christened in the local church there. Time went on and they really wanted to get back into Bideford, although they were happy in Woolsery, they were that distance away. So in their best interest and to get them on the council housing list they needed to move back into residence in Bideford. I let them move back in again.

Tracey wasn't so sure I was doing the right thing, and said so at the time. I shouldn't have really, as it was a bad time for me emotionally and the girls had still not got over losing their dad. It was a nightmare really, tempers and emotions were short and the atmosphere was at times terrible. I shut myself in my room having given up my bedroom to Michael and Elysia as it was better for them with the baby. Often I went out of the house just to be on my own and felt as though everything was falling apart. I used to escape away from the house as much as possible to Gloria's or Margaret's, or even bed and breakfast at various locations, just to get away.

On 3rd May 1997 Elysia and Michael were married at Northam registry office, and we had the reception at the Royal Hotel in Bideford. It was a beautiful sunny day, and everything went according to plan. Elysia looked so lovely in her wedding dress, and little Jade was so cute in her little dress, she couldn't walk yet but shuffled around on her bottom. We had just close family to the reception, but had a party and disco in the evening for about 100 people. Tracey was one of the bridesmaids and she looked lovely too. I tried to give them the best. Underneath, that day my heart was breaking, missing Don; he should have been there to give his daughter away. I was happy for Elysia and Michael, but I was still grieving and couldn't enjoy the day as much as, perhaps, I should have done.

When it came to Jade's 1st birthday on 30th May, it was a horrible day for me. The reason being Elysia wanted a party at the house inviting lots of people. I'd said 'no' because our house was upside down with so much of everything around half packed or unpacked. Also I couldn't face anything, really, being so depressed. Elysia couldn't see this from my point of view, so instead her and Tracey took off for the day.

1997. Elysia and Michael's wedding reception

I felt absolutely cut off and hurt. And things got even worse before Elysia and Michael were given a council house and could move out. I had said something to Elysia that came out the wrong way, and I couldn't re-track and never fully tried to explain. It didn't come out the way I mean it and she was understandably hurt. She vowed she would never speak to me again, or step into my house anymore. They left on very bad terms. So besides grieving for Don, I had the added grief of the girls' attitude. Tracey, too, was very cold to me and wouldn't speak to me half the time, and when she did it was sarcastic. At this point I felt I didn't want to live anymore. I couldn't have sunk any lower. I contemplated taking my own life, and got very close to it. Luckily I got help from my doctor, and counselling, and I got through each day. That was the only thing I could do: take each day as it came. This period of my life was the worst time ever: I was depressed for so long. Months went by and I didn't see Elysia, which meant also that I was missing out on seeing Jade, and I missed them both very much. Until one day I took the bull by the horns, and thought I'd bring the situation to a head. I went to her house and asked her if she would allow me in to talk. And that's just what we did. I said sorry and that I'd missed her; she said the same, and I knew she meant it. So it had to be a gradual thing of getting together again. I felt so relieved and so much happier. I loved both my daughters and any upset hurt terribly. Goodness knows how long this situation would have gone on for if I hadn't tackled it. It was the worse time ever in my life. It's painful to recall and I hate now having to remember this episode in my life.

By this time Tracey had decided to rent a bungalow and move out, and all our lives settled down a little. It wasn't to last long because the owner of the bungalow decided to sell and not rent out the property anymore. So Tracey was forced to start looking for alternative accommodation. It was a shame really because she had just got settled in and loved the place. Anyway nothing suitable turned up, and she moved back in again with me. It always seemed to go ok for a while before going pear-shaped again. So after a time back home, she decided to buy a house instead of renting. One such house she liked came on the market in her price range so she went for it - went ahead and bought it.

It was only the next street down. She moved in, and I thought she was at last settled, which is all I ever wanted for my girls: to be settled and happy. And Tracey worked hard to pay for her mortgage.

My life was also getting better. I felt easier in my mind and less stressed, but still grieving for Don. It would take a long time for me,accepting he was never coming back.

Before, while Tracey was still with me, in 1997, I had decided to take off on a five day break away with Wallace Arnold Coach Tours to Manchester and Stockport, visiting the fictional locations of Emmerdale, Coronation Street, and Last of the Summer Wine. It was a lovely trip and I enjoyed the break, meeting some nice people. I felt quite a lot more relaxed.

But I came back to find Tracey had had an accidential fire in my sitting room. Luckily no damage due to her quick thinking only a bit of smoke damage. It had frightened her especially as she was on her own. A crayon had found its way into the electric fire and was the cause of the fire.

The evening I had come back, I watched TV in bed and stayed awake into the early hours of the next morning. Then came the news flash that Princess Diana had been killed. It was hard to believe what was happening.

I don't know but one tragedy seemed to follow another, because after Tracey had moved out to her new house, she left her cat with me because he was old and she thought she wouldn't uproot him to a new place. Well Bobby was 14 years old and he got sick and died and again it was like losing a family member. We loved him so much.

The house was so empty without Bobby but I vowed I wouldn't get another cat. However time went on and I decided to relent. So I went to the RSPCA centre and brought another one home. This little one had been rescued, her tail had been amputated after a firework had been tied to her tail and set alight. Needless to say her tail was badly burnt and maggot-infested when the RSPCA picked her up. There were so many cats there waiting to be re-homed that I thought: 'I've got a problem here - I won't know which one to pick,' but when I came to her pen, she stood out to me. She chose *me*. It was as if she said, 'Please take me home with you.' My heart melted when I saw her, and I thought, 'she's the one.' She was so gentle and affectionate and later on she used to sense my moods and come to me if I was upset, and give me love.

She used to sleep in bed under the duvet with her head on the pillow all night, just like a child. So Skippy became a member of the May family.

After Don died I'd started going to chapel, after so many years away from religion. I felt I needed spiritual comfort. This feeling developed in going outside my religion of Methodist to the Spiritual church. I felt as I couldn't be near

Don bodily I wanted to be near him spiritually. It was at one of these meetings I was approached by a young woman who said she felt my grief wash over her as I sat next to her. We got talking and it appeared she lived in the same street as me. She offered to come to my house and give me healing. I agreed, and a couple of days later she appeared on my doorstop. She started the procedure of healing and that took a little while. She walked into different parts of the open plan room, and asked if I had any doors or windows open, as it had become cold in one part of the room. I hadn't. She then said, 'Don is here: I can feel his presence.' I crossed the room which was warm and found that one part was unusually cold. As I stood there something strange happened. My left arm from the fingertips, working its way up my arm became very warm, while my other arm from the fingertips up became icy cold. It was quite an emotional moment, very strange. After she left, and I went to bed I felt chilled right through my whole body, icy in fact. I'm sure Don was with me. I was so cold in fact that I wore my nightdress, dressing gown, and socks,with two duvets over me, and two hot water bottles, and still I was cold. It was quite an experience.

After Don's death I used to be watching TV sometimes and all of a sudden a chill would come over me, starting at my feet and working right over me, even in a warm room. It happened quite a lot and I did feel Don's presence with me.

I decided to take up art, and started going to classes, studying water colours.I enjoyed that hobby very much,it was very relaxing and found the end results very rewarding. As time went on I started into oil painting, and found I liked that much better.

I'm not sure about the dates but about this time I had started working in the North Devon Hospice charity shop in Barnstaple. I wanted to be able to give something back to them as the hospice had done a lot for Don and myself. I found I enjoyed the shop work and the company.

The car we had while Don was ill was a mobility one so needless to say it had to go back to the garage after Don died.

I was without one for a couple of weeks and really couldn't do without one. So I went back to the garage and bought it. We had it from new, so I was quite used to it, and it was so nice to have it back being the only ones that had driven it. It would be with me a total of 15 years.

On 5th June 2000, a millenium baby was born into the family: Chloe. A sweet little baby who brought her love with her. Life was sweet, with two little grandchildren, whom I adored. These were happy times, Elysia organizing her parties, christening, barbeques, birthdays etc; she loved her parties.

Michael and Elysia decided to leave their rented house and buy their own. We all had our separate lives to live now, and were not sure how the others were coping day to day.

Looking back on a happy occasion when we were all together. Elysia, myself, Donald, and Tracey

6

Nineteen ninety-nine was the year of the eclipse. I had taken note what part of which counties would be the best place to view the total eclipse. I decided to take off for the day bound for Fraddon in Cornwall where on the graphs it appeared it would be an ideal vantage point. I drove up to the downs high above Fraddon and waited for the time to arrive. There were quite a lot of people there besides me. Then it happened, the day was dry and sunny, then gradually came the darkness. As it happened the birds stopped singing. The air went still and quiet until the darkness covered everything. It was so dark you couldn't see your hand in front your face. It was quite eerie, and I'm glad I had this experience.

I was still feeling lost without Don and Tracey said she felt she needed a holiday from everyday stress and asked me if I'd like to go with her. We decided to take 2 weeks on Zante in the Greek Islands. As it happened we were lucky with the weather: it was good for the whole time we were there, even though it was late in the season. It was lovely to get away to somewhere warm, away from everyday stress.Things didn't go entirely well all the time though as Tracey was quite down and depressed; but on the whole we had a good holiday. Coming off the beach one day Tracey had bad wind-burn on her legs and we were booked in for an excursion the following day however she was in so much pain she couldn't make it. So it was decided I would go alone, and Tracey decided to stay in the bedroom and sleep. It was an all day trip that took in the whole island. I felt a bit lonely and sad on my own, but then standing outside a church I noticed a parked car with the registration DON. I don't care what anyone says, I'm sure there were signs that Don was still with me and I felt a lot better.

It was good going out to a restaurant or a tavern for a meal. I adore Greek food, and we visited a different one every evening. We found the local people so warm and friendly.

The beach was about five minutes walk from our hotel, so needless to say we took the opportunity to visit it most days. Another trip we did was to a cove where Tracey had the opportunity to go scuba diving with a group and an instructor, which I know she enjoyed. It wasn't my cup of tea, so I just relaxed on the beach until they all came back, and the sand was so hot it felt as if it were burning my feet.

The only bugbear was with the airport. It was so small and ancient it couldn't cope with the amount of people flying in and out. When leaving to fly home we had to stand outside the airport for what seemed like hours in a queue with our luggage before we could check in. When we eventually got in and checked in there was nowhere to sit, it was so crowded, wall to wall, with people. Tracey and myself sat on the floor for an hour or so until our flight was called. I hope by now the airport is updated, as I was told they had the money to do it but were too laid back to get started on it.

Anyway months went by and Tracey went through a point in her life, which would affect mine also. She had problems at work not of her own making, coming up against a sadistic bully who worked in her department. Tracey had already began to sink into a deep depression by the time we set off for Zante.

The problem wasn't sorted out and she spent another year or so in this atmosphere. Eventually she took the company to an industrial tribunal. Tracey was receiving a raw deal from life and so during this time and later on I spent all my time devoted to her supporting her as best as I could, though at times it proved to be very testing. I knew she didn't deserve this and it broke my heart to know what she was going through. Anyway I'm not going fully into that part of our life as it wouldn't be fair.

Suffice to say she decided to sell her house and move back home with me. Bringing with her all her furniture and belongings. So I had the loft chock-a-bloc, the spare room, and the cellar all filled with her things - also bringing along her, two cats. For a long time the cats didn't settle, my cat didn't want them here and there were plenty of fights. It took an awful long time to get them all used to their new surroundings, and to each other. After a while the situation improved though they still didn't like each other - I think toleration would be the word and it was the best we could hope for.

Having left her job, Tracey was broke, and feeling low. I hated to see her like this and so I booked us a holiday for two weeks in the Algarve to maybe help her feel better. It was a lovely holiday and the weather was really hot - it was ideal, and it did the trick. We stayed at a small family run hotel which had a lovely pool - very handy in the heat. It was a short taxi drive from Albufeira. Albufeira is such a pretty fishing port, having both a new and an old part, the latter I enjoyed best wandering around. We were both relaxed and enjoyed the time, sunbathing, swimming, and eating out at night. I loved the food. It was a pity it all had to end and we had to fly back.

We were back just a few days, enough time to unpack, do the laundry and pack again as we were to join Elysia, Michael, and the girls who had invited us to join them on a caravan holiday in New Quay in Wales.

This became a point in my life that became a holiday zone. Things were not altogether stress free, but I coped day by day and Tracey and I had our next holiday with a last-minute deal to Tenerife. We just wanted somewhere warm and cheap. We stayed in Las Americas, quite a nice place and we had good weather. The beaches weren't so good here, it being a volcanic island and the sand is black.

Albufeira on the Algarve. Tracey and myself in the Old Town.

We were witness to a robbery, one which happened so quickly. We were sitting on a wall by the beach facing a restaurant across the road where a lady had put her handbag on a table which was very near the road.

A lad just swiped it and ran off. A number of people gave chase but didn't catch him. We had been warned that this sort of event often happened and that we had to be vigilant.

We were self-catering this time which made a change, and the apartment was very nice. As per usual - everywhere I travel abroad - I was bitten by mosquitos, and this time I had a bite on my face. I didn't think much of the local people, who seemed unfriendly and not at all helpful.This included taxi drivers who were very grumpy and surly and shop keepers were unpleasant and unhelpful. In the places where we ate in the food was awful and not cooked properly.

So, no, I wouldn't consider going back to Tenerife anytime soon.

The following year Elysia and Michael invited Tracey and myself to go on holiday with them to spend two weeks in

Tunisia. Tracey said, 'Come on, mum, I'm going to treat *you* to this one, to say *Thank You* for everything.' I thought that was such a lovely gesture on her part. I told her she didn't have to but she was adamant she wanted to. So there you go, she booked an all-inclusive stay near the port of El Kantaoui.

The hotel was great, as was the holiday. It was lovely experiencing a different culture: the only down-side being that Arabs are so overpowering, hassle-wise in the shops, bargaining for goods, and on the streets. None of us liked that, though it cracked Elysia and Michael right up.

We did a number of excursions, one full day going up to the capital, Tunis, calling in on the way up to the 'village entirely blue.' Every single window and door of the entire village was painted blue.

Every single stop we made there was the hassle of little boy traders waving goods in our faces.

The town of Monastir was a different thing as the shops were government controlled and sold at fixed prices which was a pleasure to look around in.

Another day we took an excursion down the coast to visit an amphitheatre at El Jem, where the gladiators fought the lions. It was awesome walking around that arena, thinking about the past and the slaves that were put out in the arena to face certain death. How bloodthirsty people were. We saw all the parts where the slaves were kept, and the parts where the lions were kept before they were let loose into the big area. It's a grim history.

Going further down the coast,we were to join a pirate ship for a sail and have lunch on board. But I'm glad to say (for myself) the captain decided it was too choppy to set sail. So we had our arranged lunch on board, then rejoined our coach for the journey back. If they *had* set sail I probably wouldn't have gone with them, but would have waited in dock, after my experience in Malta.

When we first arrived to start our holiday at the hotel I was approached by a man while we were having coffee one morning out on the patio. I thought he was part of the hotel staff who asked if we'd like a free trip by mini bus to see the local shops and go sightseeing - all complimentary.

I thought it sounded lovely and suggested we all went. Well it was a con, we were driven to his family business of carpet making, leather coats, and jewellery shop, and put under a hard sell. We didn't want anything, and it was difficult as they didn't seem to understand the word 'no'. Elysia said she'd had enough and walked out, and we followed.

We weren't even sure if he was going to give us a lift back to the hotel as we hadn't bought anything, he did but he was unhappy. Elysia always reminds me of this particlar trip claiming it as 'The Day Mum Was Conned!'

The weather was really hot although it was October and we had the occasional storm. Another half-day, morning trip we went on was at El Cantuey - a camel trek. On the trek you could opt to travel by camel, horse, mule, or horse-drawn waggon. I was determined not to miss the opportunity, so I was up for a camel ride. The camels were all standing up, so we had to be thrown up on their backs by a couple of Arabs who were running the trek. The camels looked so high I thought I'll never get up there, but I did.

The trek which consisted of quite a lot of animals took us to various stops on the way so we could change if we wanted, to another animal or cart, have a rest break and enjoy local delicacy drinks and food in tents. Then it was on again to the next point. On the second point Tracey and myself opted for the covered wagon. It was driven hell for leather and I thought we might even turn over with the speed we were doing. When we got back to home base it was nice waiting for all the animals to catch up before it was time for lots of photographs. That was quite an experience, a long half day, which we all enjoyed.

One night we were driven out into the desert for a Bedouin evening, typical food, and treated to Arabian dancing. This was all staged in tents under the stars and had a lovely 'Arabian Nights' feel about it.

Six months later Tracey and myself were away again, this

2003. On the camel trail in Tunisia.

2003. Elysia and Tracey on the same camel trail.

time to Florida. Again, a last-minute deal which we'd spotted in the Travel Agents - a real bargain at £299 for two weeks, flight, and hotel. We saw the advert on the Friday, booked up immediately and flew out on the Tuesday, so it was all systems go with our packing! It was lucky our passports were all up to date. So it was Orlando here we come. We had an apartment which was part of the Holiday Inn and proved to be fine including a swimming pool. These packages are good because the airlines don't want to fly with any empty seats and have them booked up at the last minute.

Each day was packed full with the things we did. Sightseeing, shopping and of course viewing as much as possible of the Disney Parks. It was late April, early May time and very hot. We had to make sure to drink plenty of water, as we were always on the go. Being in the Disney Parks makes you feel young again whatever age you are.

Luckily the length of the flight didn't bother me over much. During the 9 hour flight, I moved around the cabin as much as possible. The older I got I had begun to be uneasy with air travel even though I had no fear at all when I was younger and in the WRNS. But now it was a different story. I think the worse flight for me had been the one back from the Algarve, my stomach turned over for the whole flight, which luckily enough was a short one. We were sitting in the rear of the plane, the engines kept making odd noises, and we kept looking at each other. My hands were literally streaming, dripping, with sweat. After each time we landed I used to think never again; I don't ever want to fly again - until the next holiday came along! I did have a session of hypnotherapy to conquer my fear,which helped when I flew again.

Six months on and I was off again with Elysia and family to Ibiza, leaving Tracey back home on her own this time. This was a real laid-back holiday and very enjoyable after a rough start. My grandchildren had picked up a bug days previous to the flight and we had quite a journey to Gatwick, stopping many times for Jade and eventually even Elysia was sick. They were all still feeling pretty rough waiting at Gatwick for our flight. Then just as we were boarding, I began to feel ill. Before we had time to take off, I was making full use of the sick bag. I was ill throughout the whole flight, going through bag after bag, even handing one to the flight attendant as we were ready to disembark. I was the last one off the flight as my legs were too much like jelly to attempt the steps. So the flight crew took me down in the lift and into arrivals in a wheelchair, I felt so weak and ill. They could have deported me to Timbuctoo and I couldn't have cared less.

On reaching the hotel I collapsed into bed fully dressed apart from shoes. Next day and the following days I gradually felt better. Not so poor little Jade, she was still quite poorly and didn't show any signs of improvement. Elysia and Michael had no option but to take her to a doctor, which did the trick, and a few days later, after some medicine she picked up and then enjoyed her holiday. We did a few trips to local markets and such but nothing on a grand scale. One glass-bottom boat we went out on in the bay was very disappointing the sea was devoid of fish or anything else. It was as if it was sterile perhaps from overfishing.

On my return from holiday Tracey and myself again had a difference of opinion and the atmosphere became tense. I think it was all due to the fact she had opted not to go with us and was left on her own for two weeks. She couldn't afford to go and she didn't believe I would go and leave her on her own.

Christmas was coming up and I was dreading it. Every year since Don died I've hated that time of year. I miss him and feel sad. So I thought this particular year I wasn't going to sit around, I would go away by myself. And that's what I did: I had five days in Eastbourne travelling with Wallace Arnold Coach Tours. It was a good idea because I enjoyed that Christmas, had a good time, and met some lovely people. I won £100 the first night there on Bingo. Tracey on the other hand had decided to spend Christmas over with Martin her boyfriend, before deciding to extend it to a couple of weeks more.

7

As time went on they decided they would give it a go living together permanently. So that was it, Tracey had moved out and began to make her home with Martin. After a while she came to visit me with the news that she was pregnant. I was pleased for her as she was so happy at this stage.

Sadly things didn't go well. During her scan at 12 weeks, she was told her baby was dead. We were all devastated - this was another blow for her. It seemed she was always fighting for the right to have some happiness. Things weren't going too well for her and Martin's relationship either at this stage and she came back home again, bringing her two cats. She was up and down with her emotions, though her and Martin were still seeing each other. They'd decided it was better at this stage to be living apart. Sometime later on she became pregnant again which lifted her spirits. But in the weeks and months to come she had quite a traumatic pregnancy, fearing all the while she would lose the baby. Well into her pregnancy she moved back in with Martin again, this time leaving her cats with me.

On September 11th 2006 baby Benjamin was born by Caesarian section, weighing 4½lbs, and began to put on weight steadily over the days to come. I held him in my arms when he was only half-an-hour old. What a wonderful moment - a little grandson. Don would have loved him. Tracey glowed in motherhood and both her and Martin adored their son. So life was good, and all the families happy.

The following April 2007 was my 70th birthday. I was told by Elysia to get dressed ready in the evening to go out for a meal. Elysia, Michael, and the girls came around to my place saying the taxi would pick us all up here. We were all ready waiting when Elysia said, 'Right! Let's go! The taxi is here!' I stepped outside and was gobsmacked to see a white stretch limo waiting. What a surprise! We stopped on the way at Instow for the driver to get out and set up a table with glasses and champagne, then it was on to Barnstaple to have our meal at the restaurant.There we were joined by Tracey, Martin, Ben, and Hannah (Ben's half sister). That was a lovely evening with all my family around me. The girls did me proud with pictures, presents, and flowers. Life was good.

Things were settling down for everyone. Martin and Tracey decided to get married and set the date for the 17th May 2008. Tracey more or less organized the whole wedding herself as she wanted to know that all the loose ends were tied up - not even letting me help. The only part she wanted me to play was in helping to choose the wedding dress.

The day of the wedding was sunny but cold. Tracey and Elysia were shivering in their off-the-shoulder dresses by the time all the photographs were taken. Tracey looked so beautiful in her wedding dress, such a picture of happiness, and everything down to the last detail was perfect. Elysia, Jade, Chloe, and Hannah were bridesmaids. Ben looked gorgeous in his little suit and cravat.

They were married in the village church at Landkey where they had made their home. Then it was on to the Royal Hotel in Bideford for the reception, carrying on into the evening for the party and disco. Martin's parents were down from Margate for the wedding and they looked after Ben while Tracey and Martin went on honeymoon to Albufeira in the Algarve. She liked the place, from when we went there years ago.

Martin and Tracey's wedding in 2008

Everybody was settled and happy. A few months later they had Ben christened in Landkey church and had the reception in the little pub in the village.

Tracey I know, was happy and was now settled. She had a little part-time job in the village shop, which she enjoyed. As she said it was a good way to get to know everyone. When he was old enough she put Ben into nursery for a few hours.

My friend Jo and I decided it was time we took a holiday, so we made the booking for December 3rd for two weeks in Luxor, Egypt. We flew out from Gatwick to Luxor to join the boat for a Nile cruise for the first week; the second week was spent in a hotel in Luxor. The first part on the Nile cruise we had many excursions. One to the Karnack Ruins in Luxor, an amazing historic site. Another was made to the Valley of the Kings during which I especially enjoyed going down into the underground chambers. Egypt has to be seen to be appreciated - all the beautiful carvings and paintings. Sometimes the

Jo and myself at the Edfu Temple of Horus in Egypt

information we had from the guides was perhaps a bit too much to take in - so much history to remember. I found it interesting culturally and we got to see all the places of interest, temples etc. The building of all the structures was so hard to fathom - how ever were they constructed? They are so tall and large and beautiful, with statues and figureheads. You can't imagine what the lives of the slaves that had to build them must have been like. The blood, the sweat and a lot of deaths. I had always wanted to see these places and found it all fascinating. Again the only drawback on the whole holiday was the hassle we received from the locals to buy their wares. They would come threateningly right up in your face and I felt intimidated and annoyed.

Although it was December and nearly Christmas it was so hot. The cruise ship was really something, it was very relaxed on board sailing along. Early on in the week both Jo and myself got a tummy upset, which I believe is called the 'Nile Tummy', and it took some time to get better, having to keep visiting the loo. We sailed the Nile as far down as Aswan, by the Aswan dam.

It was there we had an excursion by coach from the boat into the town, and dropped off at a point by a market, told to walk through, and the bus would meet us at the other end. It was about half an hour's walk, and I hated every minute, as there were locals in our face with their wares, trying to get us to buy. I just wanted to get out, while Jo on the other hand took it all in her stride and chatted and bargained with them.

The second week, we just took it easy, sunbathed by the pool, and went out of the complex in the evenings for meals in local restaurants. That was awful, as soon as we had left the complex we were approached and hassled again this time by horse and carriages. If only they realised that if they didnt hassle so much people would likely spend more. Even as we left the airport they were begging for money. I did enjoy being in a different culture and seeing all those places, but I was so glad to get on the plane and leave. I'd never go there again.

Skippy my little cat with no tail had been very ill before I left for the holiday, and I had left her with the vet. Tracey texted me the first week with the news that Skippy had been put to sleep - in the circumstances it was the kindest thing to be done, she was so ill with so many things. It broke my heart, as I'd had her for so long, and she was so dear to me.

Previous to going on holiday in that year I'd suffered chest pains that were quite severe, and was admitted to hospital for tests thinking I had heart problems, but all the tests were inconclusive, and I went home.

Before I went on holiday I had to have an operation on my shoulder after a scan had shown up that I needed to have a bone trimmed, so it was 'careful does it' with the luggage. Jo helped me a lot through the airports.

In May 2009 it was Tracey and Martin's 1st wedding anniversary, and they decided to spend a few days away together. I had the pleasure of staying at theirs, to look after Ben. What a joy, such a lovely boy, and I love him to bits.

Going on into 2009, Tracey started to get ill with different pains. Her doctor at her surgery assured her it was probably nothing to worry about, but the pains continued, and she kept going back to the surgery. She wasn't feeling very good at all but had signed up to do 'Race for Life', the cancer charity, and she went ahead and did it with Elysia and the girls, but didn't join them for lunch afterwards, but instead went straight home afterwards.

One day very soon after, while she was working at the village shop, her pains got so bad that she couldn't stand it any longer, and drove straight to A&E at Barnstaple.

I was contacted by Martin and went straight up to the hospital as I was told Tracey had been admitted to a ward. When I arrived her bed was curtained off. I asked, 'What's going on here now?' and was met with a stoney silence. Tracey looked at me and said, 'Mum, I've got cancer.' I felt sick, stunned, and couldn't believe it.

It felt as though someone had pulled the life plug. It knocked the wind out of me; I mean, it was so out of the blue. We sat there in silence trying to take it all in.

The doctors went through the procedures of what treatment could be done. They couldn't believe that someone so young - 37 years - could have stomach cancer. It was usually an older person thing. Also it had spread to her liver. If only she had been diagnosed earlier, but now it was all too late. She vowed she would fight it, and she did. She never gave in. She also said, 'I don't want any long faces around me.'

Another blow was to strike a few months later when my youngest sister died. Gloria, Nicky, and myself travelled up to Hastings for her funeral. She had been diagnosed years previously with breast cancer, but it had been treated and held back. Still, it had re-surfaced and came back. Barbara and myself had never been that close as I had moved away when she was 10 years old, and we didn't get to meet up much. She would have been 62 when she died.

So after seeing the consultants about starting chemotherapy, Tracey decided before she started, that she wanted to have a break away with Martin, Ben, and Hannah.

She wanted time away, living for the moment, while she was feeling reasonably ok. She felt once the chemo kicked in life would change, and she wanted those precious moments beforehand. She would face everything else later. They had a few days in London and met up with Martin's sister who lived there and who helped them while they were there in getting around, and had arranged a wheelchair for Tracey.

Then they travelled by Eurostar to Disney, Paris for a few more days, having booked a hotel in the complex.

Elysia, left, and Tracey during the Cancer Race For Life in 2009 - just before Tracey was diagnosed with cancer herself.

She was reasonably well and they enjoyed the trip; she so wanted her little boy to enjoy Disney. They had ten days in all away, this being at the end of October and the beginning of November 2009.

Tracey didn't really start her chemo treatment until just after Christmas. It knocked her for six, making her sick and tired. I used to go over almost every day to look after her and Ben. He was only little and didn't know what was going on him only being three and half. Not once did Tracey complain of any pain or discomfort, but bore everything bravely. She couldn't compete in the 2010 Race for Life, which upset her so much she didn't even get to watch it.

I decided I would do it that year and was going to walk with Elysia and the girls, but finished up by doing it on my own, as Elysia was not speaking to me for some reason or another.

Tracey strived to get out of the house and keep her mind off her situation, visiting and being visited by her friends. By now she had lost most of her hair and decided upon a wig. I took her to the hairdressers where they had so many styles she could choose from. The one she decided on, really suited her well,and she took to wearing a jaunty little hat as well - no-one would have guessed anything untoward, unless you knew the situation.

April came and with it my birthday. We all decided to meet up in Pizza Hut in Barnstaple, which was quite nice, and I went home with a car full of flowers.

I had an operation in May. I had been ill one particular week with severe bowel pains and by Friday they were so bad, the doctor sent me straight up to Barnstaple Hospital to be admitted, resulting in an operation on the Sunday. It turned out it was gallstones, and a cyst on an ovary. A couple a years previous I had suffered chest pains resulting going into hospital by ambulance, the tests at that time proving negative -my heart was fine. So the chest pains were likely to be referred pain which often happens. I was only in hospital a couple of days, having had keyhole surgery, so it was quick to recover.

Next month on the 26th June it was Tracey's 38th birthday. We arranged for a meal in Westward Ho! Everyone was supposed to be there. Martin's parents were down from Margate, but on the evening, Ben started playing up, so Martin's parents decided it would be best if they kept Ben at home and looked after him.

We had a good meal, and a good time, but Tracey at this stage had lost so much weight, she was so thin and gaunt, that it broke my heart to see her. The party didn't go on too long as she was so tired.

Going on into July she was struggling, her pain became worse, and she was losing weight fast. She couldn't eat much.

Ben was unaware as to what was going on.

The news was broken to us all one day when the doctor made a house call to see her. Tracey was told her time was running out, and it could be very near. It was like a knife cutting for both of us and it felt like the end of the world. She couldn't manage the stairs anymore, and didn't want to stay upstairs so she asked if she could come over to my house as I had a stairlift which I still had from when Don was ill. Also I had a shower cubicle in the bathroom which would make things easier for her. On the Saturday Martin brought her over and I settled her in. I gave her my room as it was the bigger one and more comfortable for her.

The next day Martin took her out in the wheelchair down to the park. I had been told Tracey could have palliative care, so on Monday evening the nurse came to look after her that night, so I could have some sleep. The following morning the situation had changed with Tracey. Unknown to me, in the night the doctor had been called as she'd taken a turn for the worse. I called Martin and he came over right away with Ben and I also called Elysia and Michael; the girls also came. So we were all here together with her at the end. I lay next to her on the bed and was holding her hand, when I felt a strange feeling come over me - I knew it was Don with us and that he had come to take her home with him. I said, 'Tracey your dad is here with us.' With that, there was an almighty bang which frightened us all. A picture, one of Don's, had fallen off the hook at the top of the stairs and had crashed down onto the stairlift in such a manner that it looked as though it had been just placed there.

It happened as the doctor arrived, although I hadn't called him - he was just doing his rounds. Within minutes he pronounced that Tracey had passed away.

Michael took over, and made the arrangements for her to be taken to the chapel of rest. As soon as she was gone I went straight up to her bed, it was still warm from her. I lay where she had been, and cried myself to sleep.

We had the funeral the following week, and scattered her ashes with permission in the Hospice Rose Garden with her dad's.

I miss her so very much: she was a friend as well as my daughter. There will always be a hole in my life, that can never be filled.

The next year, into 2011, I again took part in the Race For Life in memory of Tracey. This time with Elysia, Jade, and Chloe.

I can say I've had a very full life, both good and bad. Certainly not a dull life. I've tried to make the most of my life, and achieved all or most of my ambitions. I took every opportunity that was offered, and I've no regrets - and that's what life is all about.

My life was made complete by loving and having been loved by my wonderful husband Donald, who will always be with me in my heart.

Another chapter has closed and life goes on. The younger generation will soon take over.